REALISING THE POTENTIAL

A review of the future role of further education colleges

Sir Andrew Foster

November 2005

378.99

AG

39542

© Crown Copyright 2005

ISBN 1-84478-615-3

Further copies of this document can be obtained from:

DfES Publications Orderline
Tel: 0845 60 22 260
Fax: 0845 60 33 360
Email: dfes@prolog.uk.com

DfES Publications, PO Box 5050,
Sherwood Park, Annesley
Nottinghamshire, NG15 0DJ

Please quote reference code:
1983-2005DOC-EN

For more information on A review of the future role of FE colleges by
Sir Andrew Foster please visit www.dfes.gov.uk/furthereducation

Designed and typeset by Ministry of Design, Bath (www.ministryofdesign.co.uk)

Print production by Outstanding Media, Sheffield Tel: 08700 053 123

Some of the photographs in this report were supplied courtesy of the Learning and Skills Council

CONTENTS

FOREWORD BY SIR ANDREW FOSTER

Last year, I prepared a commentary on the burden of bureaucracy carried by colleges and other further education providers (*Bureaucracy Review Group for Further Education and Training, Annual Report*). The review was a powerful learning experience which left me both hopeful and concerned about the future of colleges: hopeful because of their contribution to improving significantly the lives of many and the prosperity of all; concerned about the extent to which Further Education (FE) colleges are underachieving against their potential.

The bureaucracy review addressed a number of important management themes: accountability, the inspection regime, funding flows and management information amongst them. But it was not about reviewing the big picture, and I felt that there was work left undone.

So when Charles Clarke, as Secretary of State for Education and Skills, and Chris Banks, Chair of the Learning and Skills Council (LSC), asked me to undertake a more broadly based and far-reaching review of further education I jumped at the chance. I was invited to provide advice on the key strategic issues, challenges and opportunities facing FE colleges over the next five to ten years. The aim was to identify the distinctive contribution FE colleges make to their local economies and to social inclusion, their particular mission, and what needs to happen to transform them. Do they have the capacity and capability to deliver the demands of the 14-19, skills and higher education strategies, and are appropriate governance arrangements in place to support this? The terms of reference for the Review are at Appendix 4.

Over the course of the Review, I have consulted extensively and gathered a wide range of evidence. I have commissioned research and think pieces around the key issues affecting further education, including a study of the views of over 100 learners. I have visited FE colleges and spoken to dozens of learners, staff and principals. Workshops have been held with representatives of all the major stakeholder groups including learners and employers. And I have held meetings with the all the key national players. I am very grateful for the time people have spent with me: it has felt a privilege to hear about their work. I am also grateful for the written evidence that many people and organisations have submitted.

Whilst conducting this Review many people and organisations have been keen that we should report 'what they are planning to do' especially if this action would counter well recognised deficiencies. We have been prepared to report these organisations' important intentions but the remit of this work is to 'tell it as it is'. It is well known that plans may not always succeed, and this should be born in mind in taking an evidence based approach.

I have been helped by an exceptional core group of people from The Department for Eduction and Skills (DfES) and the LSC and have greatly appreciated their support. Dr Bob Chilton, Dr Robert Smith and Dr David Martin have also made outstanding contributions throughout the programme of work.

My report sets out what I believe is a much needed vision for FE colleges and a clear set of values. One of the sector's most striking features is its diversity and reach. This heterogeneity makes it difficult to bring the essence and reform imperatives of this vital public service into focus. My report could all too easily have reflected this variety and perhaps failed to focus. I do not feel this would have helped and so have tried to limit the report's scope to the key issues that must be addressed. They are still numerous enough.

I hope you will support my analysis of the position and what is needed and, even if you do not, that you will feel I have given a balanced and objective view. I believe it offers a major opportunity for the FE colleges to take hold of their future and fully realise their potential to the benefit of all. I know many people share this vision and are eager to create a network of colleges which are proud, valued, and forward thinking.

Andrew Foster

SUMMARY

The remit for my review was to advise on the key challenges and opportunities facing Further Education (FE) colleges. Through research and extensive consultation, this report emphasises the values of greater clarity, improved leadership, organisation and management and a relentless focus on the needs of learners and business as the criteria for progress.

FE colleges can be rightly proud of their many achievements:

- over 3 million learners

- a breadth of activity including diversity, employment skills, basic skills, second chance and higher education (HE) and

- it is particularly well-positioned to facilitate social inclusion

- But there are many symptoms indicating that all is not well:

- 200,000 16-18 year olds are not in employment, education or training

- 14% of adults of working age have no qualifications

- over 5 million adults have literacy and numeracy skills below level 1

- too many students fail to achieve the qualification for the course on which they enrol

The causes of the contrast between the achievements of FE colleges and the lack of comprehensive impact are many:

- schooling shares responsibility in exporting too many failing pupils

- incorporation liberated the individual college, but failed to provide a basis for locality strategy

- there is a mismatch between the aspirations of FE colleges and available funding, but rationing decisions are either not explicit or their consequence for the displacement of existing activity is not appreciated

- persistent underperformance in some colleges and courses fails learners and damages FE's reputation

- the FE system has suffered from too many initiatives

- and, there is strategic confusion about roles, especially between the Learning and Skills Council (LSC) and the Department for Education and Skills (DfES)

- generally, FE colleges are perceived as not fully realising their potential

Above all, FE lacks a clearly recognised and shared core purpose

The way forward in resolving these causes includes:

- an appetite to catch up with competitive international economies

- a consequential core focus on skills and employability

- increasing the pool of employable people and sharing with other providers the role of enhancing business productivity

- acquiring an identifiable brand

- evolutionary, not revolutionary change

- learning from the strategic and management arrangements of other public services, both in the UK and abroad

And, in common with other public services, putting the 'user' at the centre of policy and practice. Turning 'Learner focus' from words into actions will involve:

- ensuring that all intending students receive impartial advice,

- developing financial incentives to steer students onto courses valuable to the economy,

- strengthening learner advocacy at national and local LSC level, and college level,

- offering greater choice, not only between courses but amongst learning modes

- and, in relentlessly streamlining qualifications and learning pathways

To fully realise its potential, there must be a quality imperative.

At locality level:

- underperformance by courses and a persistent minority of colleges cannot be tolerated

- a staged approach to intervention including contestability is needed

- clarity at locality level will be served by a clear and separate commissioning role built around local LSCs

- greater collaboration amongst locality providers to operate in the best interests of learners

- specialisation, as in Centres of Vocational Excellence and Skills Academies, should improve retention, results, value for money and industry support

- and the benefits of specialisation can be passed on to learners through a 'Hub and Spoke' approach to delivery

- the development of learning centres, initially located in regeneration areas, where competitive providers can outreach training into disadvantaged communities following contestable processes

And, nationally:

- seeing FE as a purposeful system, rather than as a bounded sector

- within government, the disadvantaged 'middle child' experience of FE between schools and HE needs to be repaired

- as the strategic architect of UK education, DfES should provide a coherent and managed framework spanning schools, FE and HE

- a national learning model is needed so that FE's role is constructively co-located alongside HE and schools and the effect of new initiatives is anticipated.

- the funding methodology should draw on the national learning requirement and its local components ensuring that learning activity is rewarded for impacting on those requirements

- less centralisation and moves towards greater self-regulation

- LSC's *'agenda for change'* should be supported

- simplified inspection achieved through the merger of the Adult Learning Inspectorate and Ofsted

- an improved inspection methodology that focuses on learner experience, value for money and the coherence of the locality's learning offer and impact

Within the FE system, there needs to be new collective attention to:

- converting collected information into useful systemic intelligence

- in particular, the development of a new suite of value for money indicators, using a national agency to develop them

- addressing the problems – and possibilities - of a casualised and ageing workforce and the need to improve vocational and pedagogic skills through comprehensive workforce planning

- and, there is a perennial need to invest in the next generation of college and national leadership

There is no single, 'magic bullet' solution to FE. Rather through a comprehensive set of reforms across the whole of the FE system, its power to fuel economic achievement through helping individuals realise their personal potential will provide the basis for a progressive enhancement in FE's standing and esteem in the nation's eyes.

Part 1
THE VISION

SECTION 1.1: THE VISION – REALISING THE POTENTIAL

1. The UK has a prosperous history but our future depends on our skills. The world is a competitive market and the marketplace is crowded with nations seeking to succeed. Newer entrants to the market – China for example – can call on fantastic numbers of increasingly skilful people. The world being as it is, the UK cannot assume that its future will be like its past: it truly may not be.

2. We need to maximise and fulfil the potential of all our people – young people and adults – to contribute knowledge and skills of world class quality in competitive proportion to the size of our population. Future economic prosperity and good public services depend on this.

3. The need for an outstanding FE college network is not just about national prosperity. It is also about how far countless individuals in this country value themselves, enjoy being who they are and have fulfilling and enjoyable lives. The appalling figures for the number of people who lack basic literacy and numeracy skills suggest great reservoirs of disappointment and poor self esteem. And it will surprise no one that many of those in that predicament come from the most disadvantaged parts of the community.

4. To achieve its place in the world economy, the UK needs an education and skills system that:

- Creates a pool of skilled and mobile employees.

- Provides development routes for individuals.

- Re-trains workers to keep pace with changing technology.

- Meets the needs of individuals and communities for personal and social development.

5. The Government, in its 14-19 and skills strategies, has already set out its objectives for the future.

6. The task of creating a system of 14-19 education and training matching the best anywhere requires changes to qualifications and curriculum, so that young people can learn in ways which motivate and inspire them. It also presents major challenges and opportunities for colleges. Challenges, because FE colleges are asked to expand their role further in relation to young people of compulsory school

❝ Education is the bedrock of opportunity... it is the one public policy that clearly links both our education and social values ❞

**Bob Rae, Ontario
A Leader in Learning**

age, to respond imaginatively to local needs and circumstances and to take a leading role in introducing new qualifications. But major opportunities too, to build on FE colleges' historic strengths in vocational education, to take advantage of their experience, facilities and workforce, to make the most of expanding post-16 participation and to be leaders of change in their locality.

7. For adults and employers, the Skills Strategy White Paper makes clear that colleges have a vital role in meeting current and future skills needs and improving employability. This includes increasing achievement at level 2, the basic platform for employability, and improving progression to level 3 and beyond. It sets out a range of reforms designed to help colleges and other providers improve their responsiveness to the demands of employers and learners.

THE NATURE OF THE CHANGE

8. The changes needed to create a dynamic and fully effective FE college system, able to contribute fully to these objectives and fit for the demands of the 21st Century, are not about radical restructuring of organisations or massive injections of new money. They are about the important foundations of strong leadership, clarity of purpose, clear standards with a learner focus, supportive performance management and full accountability. They are also about looking outside the FE college 'sector' and learning from best practice in other public services.

THE FE COLLEGE SYSTEM OF THE FUTURE

9. We need an FE college system – not sector – for the future which:

- Is crystal clear about and fulfils its core purpose.

- Delivers the skills the economy, businesses and individuals need.

- Consistently meets high standards of quality.

- Is held in high esteem locally, nationally and internationally.

- Looks ahead and responds to changing technological and societal imperatives.

- Is easy to navigate for learners and enables seamless progression to higher levels.

- Works alongside and in partnership with other providers and business.

- Has a purposeful, skilled, professional and inspiring workforce.

- Develops and attracts dynamic leaders.

10. We think the distinction between a system and a sector is an important one. The current emphasis on institutional groupings of providers into 'sectors', should be switched to an emphasis on learner achievement and community impact. Instead we need to see FE colleges as a vital part of a coherent system that responds to learner, societal and economic needs.

THE FE COLLEGE OF THE FUTURE

11. To achieve the positive vision set out in this report, the FE college of the future must:

- Be absolutely clear about its primary purpose: to improve employability and skills in its local area contributing to economic growth and social inclusion.

- Have a clear, well understood set of underpinning values linked to achieving excellence.

- Deliver its core purpose in an inclusive way which improves diversity and equality of opportunity.

- Command the confidence of the local community.

- Constantly strive for excellence through regular self assessment and learning from others.

- Be understood and respected by local and regional employers as providing a pool of qualified recruits with skills to meet their needs.

- Have an environment, facilities and culture which are welcoming to all learners and potential learners and take its provision out into the community.

- Regularly collect and act on learner and employer feedback. This is a priority focus for the Board of Governors.

- Be innovative and responsive to the needs of individuals and employers including reaching out into communities and workplaces and bringing learning to them.

- Have committed and professional teachers, trainers and support staff who are proud to work in FE.

- Have a profile of gender, ethnicity, age, levels of disability and sexual orientation amongst staff, managers, leaders and governors which reflects the local community.

- Work collaboratively with all local providers to meet the broader needs of the local community and improve choice.

- Be financially sound and well managed. Improving value for money is a key objective for the Board.

- Use technology in an innovative and efficient way which maximises its potential as a learning tool. Benchmark value for money datais collected, acted upon and published.

- Work effectively with its local LSC, helping develop, as well as implement, strategies.

12. We saw FE colleges which demonstrate many of these features. What is important for learners, for the economy and for social well-being is that these features become the standard for all FE colleges.

THE FE COLLEGE LEADER OF THE FUTURE

13. We also need to develop a new generation of leaders who can:

- Think strategically, creatively and systemically.

- Lead with passion, optimism and high energy, engaging and inspiring others.

- Promote a student and employer centred mission that delivers the central purpose.

FIGURE 1

Learner numbers in post 16 learning (including higher education) academic year 2003/04

Head count (thousands)

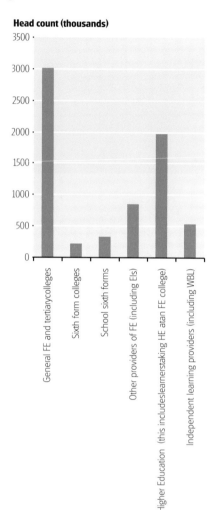

Source: DfES

failed by or have dropped out of the system, or who have not had the opportunity to participate fully in education and training. And they are playing an increasing role in **helping offenders**, both in custody and in the community, to give them key employability skills.

- Playing a central role in **supplying the skills needed for business** and economic success, engaging with 200,000 companies annually. The LSC Skills Survey shows that those businesses who use FE colleges have satisfaction rates exceeding 80%. FE colleges are major contributors to apprenticeship training.

- Addressing **the Skills for Life agenda.** Between 2001 and 2004, over 2.6 million learners undertook literacy and numeracy training and over a million people of working age have now achieved a qualification.

- Playing a key role in **14-19 provision.** Collaboration between institutions is increasing and is leading to greater flexibility at key stage 4, with pupils studying for vocational qualifications at their local FE college. Many students in years 10 and 11 are studying for AS units at their local sixth form college.

- Making a major contribution **to widening participation in higher education**, directly delivering over 10% of higher education.

- Being **flexible and adapting to changing government priorities and local needs.** Recent examples include curriculum 2000, Skills for Life, the creation of Centres for Vocational Excellence (CoVEs), the increased flexibility programmes for

14 to 16 year olds and e-learning/ **learndirect**.

- Having **a qualified, professional and highly committed workforce**.

- Focusing on **quality and excellence**. Performance across the FE college sector is improving as is the quality of leadership and management. Over the past 5 years, headline success rates have increased significantly. And 90% of provision is judged satisfactory or better.

16. These are real strengths and the FE college sector's contribution to the country's wellbeing is significant.

The un-met need

17. But despite this:

- Nearly two hundred thousand 16 to 18 year olds are not in education, employment or training.

- 14% of 16 to 24 year olds have literacy problems below level 1.

- 14% of adults of working age have no qualification.

- over 5 million adults have literacy skills below level 1 and even more have problems with numbers.

- too many communities have high concentrations of low skilled adults.

18. Leaving aside global competition, especially from Asia, the UK also has a relative problem:

- 85% of German adults and 77% of French adults of working age are qualified at Level 2 or higher compared with 64% of UK adults; and

- Only 28% of the UK workforce has intermediate skills compared with 51% in France and 65% in Germany.

19. And the situation is not static. Demographic trends bring a range of new challenges. People are living longer and the average age of the workforce is rising. The challenge will be increasingly to provide opportunities to those adults who want to gain new skills throughout longer working lives. In addition, we need to absorb new arrivals to the UK economy. Reducing numbers of younger UK born employees alongside a growing economy leads to inward migration. Although often skilled, new arrivals need these skills honing to the UK environment, their language abilities developed and their social integration enhanced.

The Leitch Review of Skills

20. In December 2004 Lord Leitch, Chairman of the National Employment Panel and formerly a Chief Executive of Zurich Financial Services, was asked by the Government to lead an independent review of skills.

21. The rationale for the Leitch Review was set out in *Skills in the global economy*, published alongside the 2004 Pre-Budget Report. Lord Leitch has been asked to consider what the Government's long-term ambitions should be for improving the UK's human capital in order to increase productivity, growth and benefits to society. The Leitch Review has also been asked to consider the policy implications of improving the UK's skills profile.

22. Issues for the Leitch Review to address are:

- The current trajectory for the development of skills in the UK and therefore the skills profile that the UK is on track to achieve in 2020.

- An assessment of whether the status quo is going to take the UK far enough, supporting productivity and growth and improving the country's comparative international position.

- The 'optimal' skills mix in 2020 in relation to promoting economic and social policy objectives and the policy implications of achieving the necessary degree of change.

23. We have met frequently with the Leitch Review team and agreed to share information and analysis and to take an integrated approach to our work.

24. The Leitch Review is due to publish its interim, analytical, report alongside the 2005 Pre-Budget Report. It will then report its conclusions and recommendations to Government in mid-2006. Further information can be found about the Leitch Review of Skills at www.hm-treasury.gov.uk/leitch.

FE Colleges: Weaknesses and Challenges

25. So the economy is a key client of an education system which needs to impart skills to the next generation, improve the ability and participation of the current generation and absorb the potential of new arrivals. FE colleges are well placed to make a decisive contribution, but are not the only player, and we say more about the wider learning and skills context later. However, with annual funding of almost £5 billion pounds they are the largest.

" After a ruined first attempt at education, Norwich City College quite literally saved me from disaster. It gave me a second chance, on opportunity to go forward with learning in an atmosphere that suited me in a way that school never could. Further Education of this kind is one of the great unsung achievements of our society "

Stephen Fry

26. There is a strong sense, very widely shared and constantly reinforced during the course of our work that, despite their strengths and achievements many FE colleges have the potential to do much more to contribute to the unmet need.

27. The particular concerns identified during the course of the review were:

- *Purpose and focus.* FE colleges are striking in their heterogeneity. They deliver in a wide variety of settings and the range of learning opportunities they present is extraordinary. Some see this variety as a strength, but there is another view that it reflects a lack of clarity about key purposes and an inefficient dilution of focus and effort.

- *Quality.* The quality of FE college delivery is monitored in various ways – too many ways, most would say. The system requires rationalisation. More importantly, although the quality of service has improved there is still significant room for improvement (for example, success rates for long vocational courses are relatively weak and vary widely by subject area and institution). The more clearly the importance of FE college work is recognised, the more determined should be the drive for excellence.

- *Image and reputation.* FE colleges have a low profile on the national stage and a relatively poor image. This is closely related to the question of focused purpose. Reputation is a key factor in the ability of the sector to attract support and resources.

- *Employer and learner influence.* Present arrangements do not provide sufficient systematic opportunities for involving key stakeholders. Too many employers do not believe that they can get from FE colleges training of the design, delivery and quality they need. According to the LSC National Employers Skills Survey in 2004, only 15% of employers make use of FE colleges when seeking solutions to their training and skills needs. And research by DfES in 2003 found that 90% of FE college principals believe that over the next three to five years their institutions will need to become more responsive to the needs of employers.

- Lateral integration and learning pathways. The complexity of local learning and skills provision means that the facilities and resources that are needed to help learners develop and achieve are not always sufficiently integrated, understood and easy to navigate.

- *FE workforce.* Until recently there has been little systematic work around workforce development. Although improving, morale is low in some areas and there are some recruitment and retention problems in skill shortage subjects and where there is competition with schools.

- *Service delivery model.* Responsibility for key management functions at national, regional and local level, particularly those involving strategy and planning on the one hand and provision management on the other, is unclear and inappropriately distributed.

- *Resource allocation*. The current system does not relate resources sufficiently closely to need.

- *Oversight and regulation*. Overall accountability and management arrangements are not fully functional and the inspection regime is complex and demanding. The landscape is crowded with a large number of overlapping bodies with either a planning, improvement or inspection role.

- *Boundary issues*. The overlap in responsibilities between FE colleges and schools, and between FE colleges and universities, leads to the potential for unhelpful competition and duplication.

- *Qualifications*. The current system is confusing and complex to navigate through.

Development needs

28. In summary, there is a lack of clarity about purpose, variable quality particularly in some vocational areas, inadequate local integration and insufficient customer focus particularly on the needs of employers. Leadership, a key driver for quality improvement, is not as good as it should be across the sector and there are an insufficient number of good managers to run highly complex college businesses.

SECTION 2.2: THE BROADER CONTEXT

Historical development of FE colleges

29. Vocational training grew greatly with the industrial revolution towards the end of the 18th century and most FE colleges have their origins in mechanics institutes or technical schools. Technological development and a culture of self-help encouraged evening classes to be set up in mechanics institutes where workers could improve their basic skills, acquire new knowledge and generally broaden their minds.

30. From this early focus on technical education, FE colleges have accumulated additional roles in offering second chance academic routes, creating opportunities for personal social advancement and inclusion, extending the delivery opportunities for Higher Education (HE) and attending to the productivity needs of employers. This accretion of roles has resulted in a rich plethora of parallel opportunities delivered mainly through GFECs. But individual FE colleges are not necessarily well placed to make choices over strategic priorities or, in isolation, to judge how well resources are used.

Incorporation

31. Incorporation in 1993 is celebrated by many as a defining moment of liberation. And in many ways it was. FE colleges moved from accountability to the locality to national accountability. FE colleges were left without clear local or national incentives or constraints. Local markets were intended to drive delivery.

32. The context in which FE colleges were given incorporated status was deliberately competitive. Unfortunately, the local learning market is a very imperfect one: learners, many of whom are the least advantaged, lack good information to guide their actions. Given the importance of FE to the economy, government was unlikely to leave this situation to continue – and it did not. Intervention through the Further Education Funding Council (FEFC), and subsequently the LSC, seemingly challenged the independent status that FE colleges felt they had attained upon incorporation.

33. FE colleges became funded by the FEFC and were required to assess local needs and meet them. The funding body lacked an explicit planning role, but through the use of funding criteria, was able to manage the pattern of learning provision. A powerful audit regime followed the funding role. Although FE colleges were intended to have a local strategic role, funding incentives strongly influenced their activity – it followed the cash. The FEFC was not organised to reflect the detail of local circumstance and so tended to focus on national objectives. The 2000 Act sought to change this situation.

The Learning and Skills Act 2000

34. 2000 saw the creation of the LSC with both funding and planning responsibilities. As well as a national office, 47 statutory local LSCs were created, enabling it to operate in local settings. As well as the majority of FEFC staff at national level, the LSC absorbed many of the old Training and Enterprise Council (TEC) arrangements and their staffing at local level. This reform clearly responded to the problems of the FEFC but, like many innovations in FE, simply layered a new arrangement on top of old systems. A typical feature of FE is the accretion of new ideas on top, rather than in replacement, of old. Consequently, in respect of local LSCs many representations suggest that they are not appropriately set up to discharge

the local planning and brokerage role, though some are very effective at this.

Strategic responsibility: The LSC and FE college roles

35. Even more serious is the potential conflict of strategic responsibility. As independent institutions, FE colleges possess the power and responsibility to develop local strategies; but now, local LSCs have an even wider strategic responsibility. Not surprisingly, there is scope for tension and conflict between individual FE colleges and some local LSCs. The local LSC arrangement was layered on top of incorporated FE colleges, without the implications for FE colleges being resolved. And FE colleges are left confused between the concepts of 'independence in what they do' or 'independence in how they do' it. FE college governing bodies have felt disempowered and directed by national priorities at the expense of local responsiveness and initiative. Despite some very strong and effective relationships in some parts of the country between FE colleges and their local LSC, we heard of examples where trust was less well developed.

36. Incorporation alone was a necessary but insufficient reform. Incorporated FE colleges need to be located within a learning market, with appropriate levels of both regulation and self-regulation that ensure that stakeholder interests are dominant. The problem with incorporation is not the freedom that it affords FE colleges in developing their delivery of learning, but that it:

- led the government and its agency into ever more interventionist roles to re-balance the market in post-compulsory education between providers and learners; and

- isolated individual teaching institutions from each other in a potentially counter-productive competitive environment, reducing the opportunities for collaborative cost-sharing, trans-provider learning pathways and the provision of learner centred advice and guidance.

37. These consequences can be mitigated, without losing the benefits of incorporation. Significant reforms are already in hand through the Skills Strategy, the 14-19 reforms, Success for All and the LSC's *agenda for change*, but more is needed to frame the country's FE college system in a fashion that maximises its impact on the nation's need for learning.

The wider learning and skills landscape

38. FE colleges form part of a wider learning and skills sector covering all publicly funded post-16 provision excluding HE. The sector includes independent providers delivering work-based learning, voluntary and community providers and school sixth forms. Whilst this report focuses on FE colleges, the answers to the problems and issues we identify have to be dealt with at the level of the broader learning and skills system as a whole. Much of the discussion is equally relevant to the sector as a totality and our recommendations will have implications for other providers operating in it.

Independent providers

39. Independent providers work directly with employers and are actively involved with over 150,000 of them. They have changed and developed over time and they play a vital role

in providing a wide variety of skills-focused learning to employers and learners. They have demonstrated significant responsiveness to employers, delivering:

- 80% of apprenticeships (200,000+).

- 60% of the Employer Training Pilots (ETP) (80,000+).

- 5-10% of FE provision via franchising (250,000 learners), dramatically widening participation.

- over 50% of Entry to Employment (E2E) provision.

40. Many FE colleges already work closely with independent providers to deliver packages of training to meet employers' needs. We need to see more of this. The Government's Skills and 14-19 strategies require far greater flexibility and employer involvement in the design and delivery of vocational training and this will mean using the acknowledged strengths of the different types of provider in the sector.

Voluntary and community providers

41. Within the learning and skills sector there is also a vital role for voluntary and community organisations. They have their roots in local communities and can reach out to sectors of the population that may, for whatever reason, not wish or be able to take part in more formal learning. They have an absolutely crucial role in opening up learning opportunities for those without qualifications and those facing disadvantage. Again, we saw some excellent examples of where collaboration with FE colleges was providing flexible and supported progression from non-accredited to learning at higher levels and this must continue.

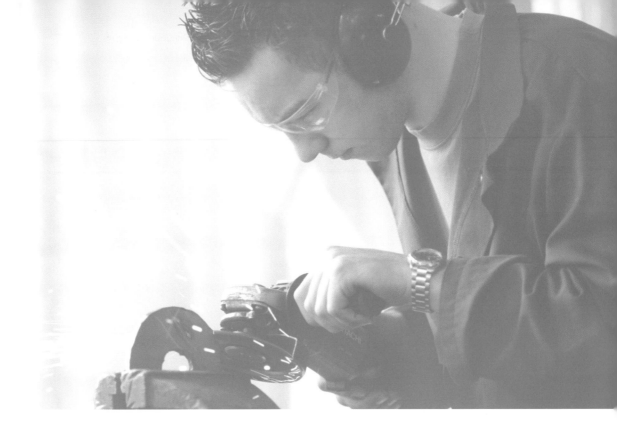

Part 3
THE ACHIEVEMENT IMPERATIVES

SECTION 3.1: THE PURPOSE IMPERATIVE

42. There are no fully shared views on the purposes of FE colleges and a key theme of this report is that this must be rectified. The confusion reflects the historical development of the sector.

43. Over time the FE college sector has responded to the ebbs and flows of need, funding and policy, acquiring but not necessarily shedding responsibilities and developing a multi-purpose culture and image – not rectified by the 1992 reforms.

44. The range of potential roles for FE colleges far exceeds what can be funded and the mismatch of possible (and actual) roles compared with need and funding is at the heart of the FE dilemma. It is the key reason why FE colleges are confused about their role

and feel under-funded in relation to their task.

45. Some see diversity of activities as a strength but it leaves others with the impression that FE colleges lack clear themes that interested partners can identify with. Many potential champions in business and government find it difficult to relate to an FE college network with such a wide portfolio of activities.

46. There is a great need to focus more selectively and strategically, finding the sector's true role and place in the education system as a whole.

A 'purposes map'

47. The sector's activities can be grouped under three, sometimes overlapping, main purposes:

- *building vocational skills* – providing a range of courses and qualifications to prepare learners for employment and upskilling those in the workforce.

- *promoting social inclusion and advancement* – delivering courses that meet learners' personal aspirations or promote social integration.

- *achieving academic progress* – including GCSE and A level work, often 'second chance' and providing vocational, as well as academic, pathways to HE.

48. To complicate the picture, these purposes may be expressed differently by or for different learner age groups, who often need different teaching and learning approaches. But the range of purposes and the range of recipients are generally brought together in a

FIGURE 2

Levels of adult literacy
Our levels of basic adult literacy in the UK lag behind those in many other countries.

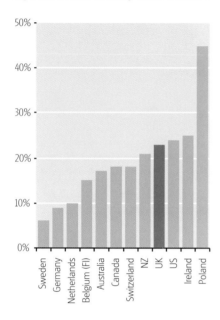

Source: DfES
Note: Proportion of the 16-65 population at lowest literacy level, IALS (OECD Education at a glance, 2000).

common institution – the FE college. This conflation gives FE an indistinct 'brand' image. FE colleges lack a clear profile which employers and other stakeholders can buy into. The accretion of activities provides variety of opportunity but also conveys a confusing lack of focus and obscurity of core purpose.

49. Moreover the picture is not stable over time. The Government, either directly or through the LSC, from time to time pursues initiatives to which it gives priority. As a responsive and adaptable sector, FE colleges react – usually in pursuit of target driven funding. But because human, financial and physical resources are spread thinly, priority emphasis in one area has a 'cuckoo in the nest' effect elsewhere. Priority activities are achieved, but the opportunity cost can be a reduction in other services, opportunities and commitments.

50. For example there are widely held views that in recent years:

- Attention to the youth cohort has focused activity away from adults.

- Concentration on level 2 activity has reduced higher cost level 3 work.

- The focus of public funding on qualifications has steered FE colleges away from non-qualification courses and many colleges have not found it easy to develop bespoke offerings for employers.

51. The indistinct profile that results from the variety of provision and from policy shifts is further blurred by wider trends. HE is taking a broader role as it reaches for its 50% participation target. FE colleges are also being drawn increasingly into school-level

activity, rescuing young people whose schooling experience has been unsuccessful. But at the same time, the arrival of vocational specialist schools potentially duplicates their role as the initial provider of vocational education.

52. So, in a changing landscape, the FE colleges are more and more drawn and squeezed into roles that are defined by demographic and policy changes and the emerging roles of HE and schools.

Regaining focus

53. As mentioned earlier, the case for FE colleges to play a more significant and focused role in meeting national economic and social objectives is compelling. To remain a world class economy, the UK needs world class assets and, amongst these, human capital is cardinal. But at the moment the capability of the UK population to achieve its full economic potential is constrained. CBI Employment Trends (2004) indicates that skills shortages have a serious business impact on 24% of employers, with only 14% reporting no problems.

54. In response, the UK education system needs to:

- Improve the ability output of secondary schools. This is a major task as currently 50% of young people in England do not achieve Level 2 by age 16. Only 54% of young people gained 5 or more GCSEs at grades A* to C in 2004 and just 44% gain 5 or more GCSEs at grades A* to C including maths and English. (The point will not be laboured unduly, but the task facing FE colleges is as great as it is partly because the multi-billion pound schools system underperforms.)

- Improve the employability and commitment to employment of UK adults including improving literacy and numeracy **[FIGURE 2]**.

- Address our major weaknesses at level 2 **[FIGURE 3]**.

- Upskill the current workforce, where there are particular problems around intermediate and higher level skills (recognising that there will continue to be a need to replenish skills in those occupational areas where demand is decreasing) **[FIGURE 4, overleaf]**.

- Absorb new arrivals to the UK economy.

The fundamentals: skills

55. The potential value of the FE sector should arise from its contribution to the success of the economy, employers and individual learners. Only secondarily is it about the success of FE providers and those who manage and regulate them. We need a simple revisitation of purposes and values, and clear priorities, so that the system may be re-engineered around them.

56. Amongst the three broad categories of FE activity mentioned earlier (building vocational skills, promoting social inclusion and advancement, and achieving academic progress), where should the emphasis be placed?

57. Although the diversity of the FE offer is often celebrated, it became clear during the review that many stakeholders believe the unique core focus of FE should be in skill building for the economy. This is the tradition

from which much of FE developed, but it is a tradition that has been diluted in recent years. We therefore propose that skills, an economic mission, is the route for FE, but interpreted in line with values of opportunity and inclusion which matter so much to those who work in FE. A focus on vocational skills building is not a residual choice but a vital building block in the UK's platform for future prosperity. It gives FE colleges an unequivocal mission and the basis of a renewed and powerful brand image. Recent reviews of FE in Northern Ireland and Ontario, Canada, have come to similar conclusions (see Appendix 2 for information on the Ontario review).

58. It is not suggested that skills development is the only thing that FE colleges should pursue. The other pillars of social inclusion and advancement, and academic progress, are not invalid. The important thing is to recognise and focus on the core purpose and have declared, clear priorities. In any event it is absolutely

FIGURE 3

Population that has attained at least upper secondary education (2003)

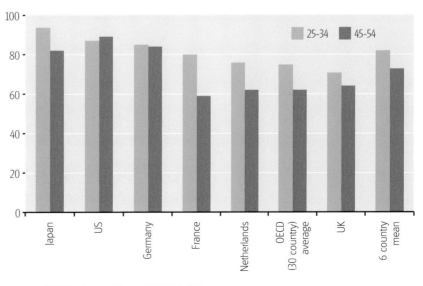

Source: OECD, Education at a Glance 2005, Table A1.2a

FIGURE 4

Projected changes in occupational structure between now and 2012

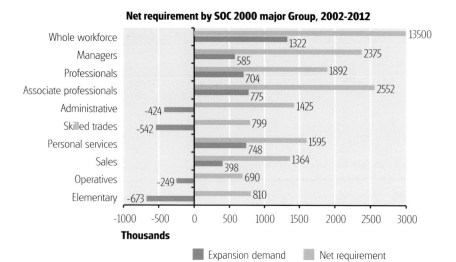

Net requirement by SOC 2000 major Group, 2002-2012

■ Expansion demand   ■ Net requirement

Source: derived from table 5.1 in Working Futures National Report

clear that an emphasis on skills development will itself turn out to be a huge driver for social inclusion and improved personal self esteem, achieving a valuable synergy between societal and personal need.

Leisure and personal development learning

59. What does this mean for non core activities including learning for leisure and personal development purposes? Such learning must remain a valuable and important part of overall lifelong learning. However, recognising its value does not mean that all colleges should provide it, or that the Government must pay for it in full. In some areas, especially where the FE college is the only adult provider, colleges must continue to play a role in providing personal and community development learning. The local LSC and local authorities must work together with other local partners such as libraries, museums and the voluntary sector

to ensure that a vibrant, flourishing and diverse range of personal and community development opportunities exists locally and is appropriately supported. A clearer vision and focus for FE colleges will in turn help other providers of personal and community development learning to in turn define themselves by contrast.

Key steps in achieving this new focus

60. We believe that in order to deliver this skills focus, as an imperative, a number of important things need to happen. The hallmarks of a skills focused FE system will be:

● Mission statements of GFEC and tertiary colleges which are absolutely clear about this core business. Many mission statements, particularly those of GFECs, at the moment are not. Their statements say much about the college's values and the comprehensive nature of its provision, but generally do not directly articulate a skills focus. The Chairs and governors of FE corporations have an important responsibility for determining the educational character of their organisations. We recommend that GFEC and tertiary college corporations look closely at their current mission statements, realign them around skills and work through the many implications of doing so (including looking at the scope for developing vocational specialisms). We also think the Government, in consultation with the sector, should consider whether any changes are needed to the Instruments and Articles of FE colleges to underpin this new focus.

- A continued drive on the development of vocational specialisms within colleges, supported by funding incentives, as a key way to improve the quality of vocational learning and strengthen engagement with employers.

- A clear capital investment strategy which supports this focus on skills. This strategy must prioritise capital projects which improve the skills focus, including incentives for greater vocational specialisation. We say more later about the way we expect capital to be used as a lever for reform.

- A performance management system which recognises and rewards skills development and the contribution to economic growth. This will include performance measures and benchmarking data which looks at impact and outcomes linked to the core purpose. More is said about this in the Quality Imperative section.

- College workforce and leadership development programmes which encourage and incentivise investment in developing the competencies to deliver this core purpose. More is said about this in the Quality and Workforce sections.

- A tough approach to poor quality provision. Colleges must improve or close down areas where provision is not giving learners the skills and experience they need to succeed. More is said about this later.

- Employers purchasing increasing volumes of services from FE colleges and having confidence that their local college provides a good source of recruits with the necessary skills. The LSC's *agenda for change* proposals will help by establishing a new national kitemark of excellence which tells employers about the quality of services provided. It will be vital that this new quality mark is developed with business.

Developing specialisms

61. We think there is much greater scope for GFECs to develop specialisms to support improved vocational education and skills development. This trend has already started through the successful CoVE programme, which needs to be developed further. We saw examples of how the best CoVEs have built close partnerships with business and are disseminating best practice to other FE colleges across the network.

62. Implementation of the 14-19 reforms will also require FE colleges to play a central role in the delivery of the 14 specialised diplomas. This will be important to ensure that young people gain sound foundations for employment, but also have the skills local employers need. The development of vocational specialisms will enable FE colleges to carve out a distinctive role for themselves within local 14-19 partnerships.

Skills Academies and CoVEs

63. The new Skills Academies, working with Sector Skills Councils (SSC) and the LSC, offer an exciting opportunity to develop in a systematic way across the country networks of specialist provision with a focus on raising vocational standards and meeting employer needs. As they are established, Skills Academies will have the resources and expertise to build and maintain curriculum and qualifications that are in line with contemporary sector needs. They should become the national

centres for excellence, and establish clear networks connecting to CoVEs at local and regional level and to local departments in FE colleges. As well as providing materials, curriculum support and best practice, this hub and spoke model would also strengthen opportunities for staff development including industry skills updating.

64. These vocational hub and spoke arrangements will require clear planning and management arrangements to ensure strong links are established with all colleges offering provision in that sector across the country. It seems right the Skills Academies have a leading role, and are accountable to the relevant SSC for their success.

65. Until Skills Academies are established in every sector, a successful CoVE might be nominated to act as the coordinating hub in the interim. However, as the initial focus of the CoVE network was on vocational skills at Level 3, this CoVE would need to meet a broader set of quality tests. Indeed, we recommend that this hub and spoke model would be strengthened by a re-branding and re-accreditation of the whole CoVE network to a new set of standards so that they can become local or regional centres of vocational excellence for their sector, covering expertise in the full range of learning offers that business and learners need, including apprenticeships. It will be critical to engage and consult with SSCs (who should have a significant role in the development of the CoVE network) and with colleges and other providers in developing this new standard and the hub and spoke mechanisms. It will also be important that these proposals are linked to the LSC's new quality mark.

Sixth Form Colleges

66. We have given a lot of thought to the position of sixth form colleges within the FE college system. Inspection evidence, high learner satisfaction rates, higher than average success rates and significant numbers gaining Beacon status, all point to sixth form colleges being a very successful model for 16-19 provision. They have a distinctive and clear mission, which is primarily focused on academic achievement and progression, and is well understood and respected by the general public. Sixth form colleges are able to generate genuine choice for young people because the scale of their operations enables them to sustain broad curriculum options.

67. We believe that it is important to protect this distinctive brand, and to ensure that it continues as a high quality option for young people with the aspiration to progress through academic pathways either to employment or higher education. But we heard many representations from sixth form colleges that treating them in policy and operation terms in the same way as general FE colleges and tertiary colleges, puts at risk their distinctive ethos that has contributed so much to their success. We are also concerned that the inclusion of sixth form colleges in the FE college 'sector' (as a brand) would dilute attempts to focus colleges on core vocational purpose.

Sixth Form college governance

68. We are not proposing that we change the governance arrangements and associated flexibilities which sixth form colleges gained on incorporation. We heard many representations that the freedom given in the 1992 Act

has allowed each college to develop according to the environment in which it is situated. But we believe that they should be treated as a distinctive institutional model, and their results recorded separately in official statistics. We also feel that this distinctiveness should be reflected in the way policy is applied and operational changes are implemented, including the recommendations in this report. In particular to achieve this, we recommend that within the DfES and the LSC, policy development and implementation is informed by a stronger managerial focus on the role and contribution of sixth form colleges. We would expect this to lead the removal of any barriers to market entry for new sixth form colleges, in the same way that barriers to new school sixth forms have been removed.

Higher level skills

69. The contribution of colleges to both progression and delivery of higher level skills is absolutely essential, but this role is not yet widely recognised. This is absolutely central to the renewed skills purpose we propose in this report. There are far fewer progression opportunities for learners in many vocational programmes than for those following the academic route. 90% of those on conventional A level programmes enter higher education, but only around 40-50% of those qualifying at level 3 on vocational subjects do.

70. FE colleges in England contribute more than a third of undergraduate entrants to higher education (indeed they are the main route for adults and for entrants from lower socio-economic groups). They are absolutely essential

to the Government's drive on widening participation in higher education. We must continue to bring down the walls between FE colleges and universities if we are to open such opportunities to everyone.

71. There are some excellent examples of collaborative partnerships between HE and FE colleges across the country, including the Lifelong Learning Networks (LLNs). At the core of every LLN is the aim to:

- bring greater clarity and certainty to progression opportunities;

- develop the curriculum as appropriate to facilitate progression; and

- ensure learners can move between different types of vocational and academic programmes as their interests and needs develop.

72. There are currently some 30 LLNs at various stages of development. They centre around developing progression agreements between the FE and HE partners and typically will link together colleges and universities across a city, area or region. These collaborative arrangements are still at an early stage of development, but their extension nationally, in due course, will be important to ensure that pathways are established for all learners onto higher levels of learning, including those following work-based routes. The Review saw in the US, excellent examples of collaborative arrangements between community colleges and their university partners, underpinned by very clear progression routes **[BOX 1, overleaf]**. Indeed, community colleges are integral to the American higher education system, and their collegiate functions are key to their

> 66 *I also thought... because I wanted to go to university, that it would be more beneficial to go to a different institution before then going to university, rather than staying on in school. I think that would have been a bigger leap, so I wanted to come and meet new people and new teachers, and start again really.* 99
> **Young female studying full time**

> 66 *...if you go on to university [without going to college] it's going to be like a big step, because you haven't had the college bit in the middle.* 99
> **Young female studying full time**

BOX 1

Pathways and Progression in US Community Colleges

- Community colleges in the US belong to a high esteem system alongside universities and this enables clear pathways and progression routes for learners. The Associate Degree, acts as a high status credit framework within which most community college students take courses.

- The two year Associate Degree is a very significant part of degree education and enables a route towards a degree in community colleges that offer local provision with open access.

- These collaborative arrangements enable learners to progress easily into higher levels of learning.

missions. And improving collaboration between colleges and universities is a key feature of the Ontario review – 'A Leader in Learning' (see Appendix 2).

73. FE colleges also have a major role in delivering HE. They provide over 10% of HE and teach one in nine of the undergraduate population. However, the 'special mission' for sub-degree, predominately vocational HE, accorded to colleges following the Dearing Inquiry to Higher Education in 1997 has been a source of unease in both the HE and FE sectors. There are concerns about mission stretch and policy overload particularly in large GFECs where provision spans from pre-entry level to degree programmes. The parallel system of higher education in Scotland is different as colleges have responsibility for a discrete level and style of higher education and where higher education institutions provide all first degree and post graduate provision. This has contributed to significant growth in higher education in Scotland. However, we also recognise that there are examples of excellent sub-degree provision in universities as well as colleges. There is not a clear cut blue print.

- The Government articulates a core role for the FE colleges, in particular GFECs, in supplying economically valuable skills. General FE, tertiary and specialist colleges should adopt as their primary purpose improving employability and supplying economically valuable skills.

- The Government recognises that a primary focus on skills does not exclude other significant purposes in promoting social inclusion and facilitating progression.

- The Higher Education Funding Council for England (HEFCE) and LSC, colleges and universities should expedite work to ensure clear learner pathways exist across the country to enable progression to higher levels.

Equality, diversity and social integration

74. As we said earlier, a skills focus will help FE colleges' commitment to, and role in, facilitating social justice and integration. FE colleges have a strong commitment to social inclusion and inclusive learning. They have responded positively to the push from Government to widen participation and tackle the country's basic skills deficiencies and have created the infrastructure to deliver "first rung" and other non-traditional provision for a whole range of disadvantaged groups. They have been particularly successful in helping to achieve government targets for basic skills and have an increasing role in learning for offenders both in custody and in the community.

75. As a result they attract a higher proportion of disadvantaged learners than the local population average.

- 56% of 17 year olds in full time education in GFECs come from the bottom 3 socio-economic groups compared to 31% in sixth form colleges and 22% in maintained school sixth forms.

- 29% of learners in GFECs are from relatively disadvantaged postcode areas compared to 25% in the population as a whole.

- 14% of FE learners are from non-white ethnic groups compared to 8% in the overall population.

- 8.2% of learners in GFECs and 6.2% in sixth form colleges have a declared disability or learning difficulty (spread widely across college network).

76. This is an immensely valuable role which meets both economic and social needs.

77. We heard a great deal about the important role colleges have in their community in supporting social mobility and social justice and in being instrumental in raising aspirations for those that have been failed by, or dropped out of, the system. Demographic changes and an increase in local diversity will mean that the number of learners from under-represented groups is set to increase and colleges will need to adapt to their changing requirements.

78. We heard of a number of examples of colleges working with local community and faith groups and adapting their provision and teaching to meet the needs of different groups. We also heard that many students learn more effectively in an environment which reflects the culture and diversity of the communities in which they live. Minority ethnic groups are significantly concentrated in five areas: London, Birmingham, Manchester, Leeds/Bradford and Leicester (identified in the National Employment Panel report on minority ethnic employment) and colleges need to be a key part of focused effort in these areas to develop strategies for engaging with and supporting people from different groups and to integrate local employment and skills systems.

Learners with learning difficulties and/or disabilities

79. It is also important that learners with learning difficulties and/or disabilities have access to a better choice of high quality provision to meet their needs. We welcome the review, commissioned by the LSC, being led by Peter Little on the LSC's funding and planning of provision for learners with learning difficulties and/or disabilities. The review has found that the needs of most of these learners can be met more appropriately and in a more cost-effective manner locally. The review recognises that the LSC cannot be the sole funding agency for these learners where there is a need for collaborative packages that include specialist care, health and other types of support. Of concern to us is the finding that the quality of provision for this group of learners remains variable. We support the overarching recommendation of the review that the LSC should develop a national strategy for the collaborative regional/local delivery of provision for learners with learning difficulties and/or disabilities that is high quality, learner centred and cost effective.

66 *Everyone merges in, even though they are so diverse.* 99

Young female studying part time

66 *I'm not really from England, I've only just come over here two years now, I didn't have the opportunity where I was, now I have it so I'm going to take it. To get into further education means a lot. If you can take the opportunity that you've got and make something out of it, I think that's brilliant.* 99

Young male studying full time

> 66 *I'm learning quite a bit and I'm still learning. You know, people think 'oh, I've done that so I'm alright now.' But you're not because there's still more you want to learn in case you want to get another job or something. Because everybody changes their jobs around quite a bit and that helps to change your jobs and that.* 99
>
> **A young female studying part time**

Governance and top management roles

80. One particular area of concern to us was the marked under representation of black and minority ethnic groups in governance roles and top management positions. The workforces of FE colleges are still seriously unrepresentative of minority groups compared to the profile of its learners, particularly at senior levels, and this restricts progress in colleges and impacts on culture. There are currently 9 (2.3%) chairs of governors and 7 (1.8%) principals from minority ethnic groups, and the position at lower and middle management is also problematic for succession planning. There are so few black and minority ethnic staff at middle manager level, that it will take a very long time for more staff from under represented groups to reach senior positions, without a fast track programme that has credibility. Just as startling is the complete absence of any minority ethnic presence on the senior management teams of all the key national organisations in the system including DfES, LSC, AoC, Ofsted, CEL, ALI, ALP, LSDA and ACM and only a small number on the boards of these organisations. The picture is rather better on women at senior levels and there is no data for those with disabilities. Progress is being made through initiatives such as the Network for Black Managers (NBM) to influence policy makers and leaders in the system but more needs to be done to better reflect the population in which colleges are operating. Workforce training, such as that developed through the Black Leadership Initiative needs to become more widespread.

WE RECOMMEND

- The Learning and Skills Council should give consideration to implementing the recommendations of its review by Peter Little of learners with learning difficulties and/or disabilities.

- An independent organisation should review the recruitment processes for Chairs of FE colleges to assess their effectiveness and make recommendations to the Government.

- The Learning and Skills Council recruits the services of a senior executive search firm who will specialise in strengthening the numbers of employees from diverse backgrounds coming forward for competitive interviews in non-executive and senior management roles.

- The Centre for Excellence in Leadership (CEL) and other partners should expedite and augment the Black Leadership Initiative and the outstanding recommendations of the Commission for Black Staff in FE.

- The Learning and Skills Council should support general programmes of diversity awareness training within colleges.

SECTION 3.2: THE QUALITY IMPERATIVE

81. Articulating a skills focused purpose, a sense of priority, a clearer message, is part of the task. Another is the pursuit of quality in the services provided to implement it. Tackling the quality imperative means understanding the impact of services,

whether they achieve what is desired and also whether services are delivered in an efficient, cost effective way. It also means paying determined attention to learners' and employers' views and the value of what is provided to meet them.

82. Much of the rest of this report is about the management arrangements needed to support a skills focus and high quality, and about how to bring about change. This section is about various dimensions of the journey towards quality and impact.

83. Significant reform is already happening or planned to improve quality. Continued implementation of the Success for All reforms, changes planned through the LSC's *agenda for change* five-point plan for quality, and the establishment of the Quality Improvement Agency (QIA), are starting to bring greater clarity in the quality infrastructure and the development of a culture of self improvement in colleges. Moreover, on many occasions individuals and groups have told us they have reforms planned in this area. Nevertheless, we have concentrated here on the situation we have actually encountered on the ground.

Quality assessment

84. The formal assessment of quality in FE colleges is based on three measures: inspection evidence, learner success rates, and learner satisfaction levels. As we said earlier, headline success rates have increased. But these national increases mask poor performance in a number of vocational subjects. Retention and achievement rates vary significantly by vocational subject area and there has been little narrowing of the performance

gap between the best and worst colleges over the past six years. Real future improvements will have to be demonstrated in continued increases in long course vocational success rates.

85. The current system is also overly reliant on inspection grades and success rates and emphasises institutional output targets. It does not measure outcomes or relate outcomes to inputs; there are concerns about what is meant by quality and how it should be measured. It seems to us that quality cannot be fully defined (or measured) without greater clarity of purpose of the kind advocated and without taking account of actual outcomes or impact. In other words, colleges must stretch for higher quality in the work they do, but look to see the fruits or measure of it in real economic and social changes closely related to priority objectives.

86. To provide more rounded measures of quality, new measures of success are being developed by the DfES, LSC and inspectorates over the next two to three years. These cover equality and diversity, learner satisfaction, value for money and responsiveness to employers. And there is work being led by Learning and Skills Development Agency (LSDA) on public value which is looking at the contribution made by public services to economic, social and environmental well-being. This has the potential to provide more dimensions that are wider than those normally measured through performance targets. But to support the renewed focus for colleges on vocational skills development, these new success measures must, as a priority, include measures of success based on employability, raising skills levels and impact in the workplace.

87. Using these new measures of success, and broader indicators of impact, the LSC needs to press on with its plans to develop a set of benchmarks, which should form the basis of self assessment and, ultimately, a self regulation system.

Value for money

88. Also, the current system does not look at how effectively colleges utilised resources. We were unable to find useful data on these issues. While many other public services have streamlined their approach to procurement to achieve significant cost savings, little progress has been made in FE and the LSC needs to progress quickly it plans under the business excellence theme of *agenda for change*. There is a strong case to launch a range of value for money reviews on issues such as asset utilisation and procurement.

Self Regulation – a medium term goal

89. It is important to make a distinction between the need to prove quality and the need to improve it. Currently, the rigours of proving the quality of provision to the plethora of interested bodies, including qualification bodies, are in danger of detracting from the need for continuous improvement and the ownership of that by FE colleges. (We say more about having to deal with a plethora of awarding bodies in section 5.3).

90. The key responsibility for quality improvement rests with colleges themselves. Self assessment, based on

quantitative and qualitative measures that are tested with the customer and conducted through rigorous benchmarking and peer review, is the way forward for colleges. However, this must be supported by high quality national support programmes, developed in partnership with colleges.

91. We welcome the work being taken forward by the Association of Colleges (AoC) on self regulation. This should build on the assessment framework that forms the basis for inspection and is being developed by the LSC through its *agenda for change*. This should be informed by best practice in other public sector services including the local government improvement model. There should be a central role for FE college governing bodies and should include value for money measures and benchmarks. It should be rigorous and effective and include value for money measures and benchmarks.

Comparison with other regimes

92. We were very struck that several other effective systems that we studied do not have anything like the same large scale regulatory, inspection and advisory system. We saw examples of how self regulation worked in the USA [BOX 2] and how a credible peer assessment system can result in trusting colleges to regulate themselves without heavyweight accountability systems weighing down on FE colleges.

93. The medium term vision must be that stage by stage we move to a system in which local colleges which are locally responsive, demonstrate excellence to learners and employers, and value for money, are rewarded with increased freedoms and flexibilities. This will energise and

motivate local staff, cost less and give excellent results.

94. A mature self regulation model however is some way off for colleges in this country, as concerns about quality and impact remain in the here and now. More conventional quality approaches must continue to be refined and their application strengthened.

Quality Improvement

95. Ofsted has, very positively, identified some of the characteristics of successful colleges **[BOX 3, OVERLEAF]**.

96. This material provides a convincing basis for improvement action and should be taken up by the QIA in developing its quality improvement strategy and in the LSC's approach to quality assurance and planning.

97. Improving teaching and learning is a priority area. High quality teaching and learning has a major impact on the quality of the learner's experience and on learner outcomes. Inspection evidence confirms excellent practice in many institutions, but there is a resistant tail of inadequate teaching. Almost half of all GFECs have at least one curriculum area that is unsatisfactory at inspection. There are pockets of poor performance in a number of vocational areas: construction, engineering and foundation levels.

Improving teaching and learning

98. The Government is currently tackling concerns about teaching and learning in a number of ways including important changes to initial teacher training. It has also established a long-

BOX 2

SELF REGULATION: A United States regional model

The system

- The Middle States Commission on Higher Education (MSCHE) is one of 6 regional accrediting associations of degree-granting colleges and universities in the US covering over 500 institutions. The MSCHE is a voluntary, non-governmental, peer-based membership association dedicated to educational excellence and improvement through peer-evaluation and accreditation.

- Accreditation is a means of self–regulation and peer review of the institution as a whole and is a voluntary process. Once accredited, institutions agree to abide by the standards of the MSCHE and to regulate themselves by taking responsibility for their own improvement. Accreditation by the MSCHE is an expression of confidence in the institution's mission and goals, its performance and its resources.

- The accreditation process is mission-based and starts with the purpose of the community college and student outcomes. Focus and planning are then related to that. Accreditation is based on the results of an institutional review by a team of peers assigned by the Commission. The trained team of 8-10 evaluators are from similar colleges and universities and an institutional visit usually takes 3 days

- Institutions must demonstrate that they meet 14 standards for accreditation that are grouped under institutional context and educational effectiveness The standards relating to students learning and outcomes are viewed as the most challenging by community colleges. The Commission determines whether an institution meets the accreditation standards based on evidence presented by the institution in its self study process.

- Colleges are evaluated every five years and the most comprehensive evaluation occurs ten years after the institution is initially accredited. When an institution fails to meet the Commission's standards, a range of actions can follow. These include warning an institution that its accreditation is in jeopardy, placing it on probation and requiring it to show cause why its accreditation should not be removed. The findings of the MSCHE are made public and this is a powerful lever for improvement.

For more information on the MSCHE system, see www.msche.org

term national change programme (Success for All) which focuses on priority subject areas. There are three key elements: developing world class teaching and development resources; training for subject champions in coaching skills and a subject coaching network to share good practice. The programme is helping to build long-term capacity to improve subject teaching.

99. Evaluation of the first four pilot curriculum areas addressed is showing

Why colleges succeed: Ofsted

A report based on a study of 29 highly successful colleges, constituting 8% of the total colleges inspected between April 2001 and June 2004. They comprise 17 sixth form colleges, 9 GFECs or tertiary colleges and three specialist institutions. In all cases, percentages of teaching and learning are well above the benchmark for the type of institution in question. All the colleges were awarded a grade 1 (outstanding) for leadership and management, had an average curriculum grade of at least 2.1. In all cases, financial management is excellent, as is their value for money. They all had the following judgements in common:

- Very good retention and pass rates

- Highly effective teaching

- Extremely successful learning

- Excellent support and guidance for students at all stages in their programme

- An exemplary response to educational and social inclusion

- Outstanding strategic leadership and governance

- Consistently good curriculum management

- Rigorous quality assurance processes which include accurate self-assessment, a detailed and regular focus on classroom practice and effective performance management of staff.

Geographically, these 29 colleges are located in all parts of the country, with 14 in the north of England and 15 in the south. These colleges are not restricted to affluent areas.

increased learner motivation, improved learner engagement and good levels of satisfaction with the materials and approach being developed as well as increases in success rates. Early evaluation shows that good practice from these pilots is being embedded across the FE colleges. What is needed is the development of a sustainable, long-term culture of continuous improvement in teaching, training and learning. The extension of this programme to other key areas will be important. Long term continuous improvement will require the commitment of teachers/trainers, institutions and providers, as well as government agencies and policymakers.

Improving vocational and subject expertise

100. Improving teaching and learning is also about subject relevance. Teachers and managers need to ensure that those who came into FE colleges with expert technical skills are enabled to keep those skills up to date. Representations from business suggest that some teachers do not have a sound understanding of the latest industry developments. Many colleges have substantial budgets for continuing professional development but it has been said that activity often concentrates on generalised teaching competence rather than subject and technical pertinence. FE maintains its relevance partly by employing part-time teachers who are also current practitioners. But more secondments between industry and education could help too. Additionally, sabbaticals for long-term full time lecturers, and indeed some support staff, back in to industry would help to update skills.

The hub and spoke arrangements which are needed to underpin greater specialisation across the FE colleges will also help as they will provide broader regional and national opportunities for such secondments.

101. But we believe we need to go further than this voluntary, mainly FE college- driven approach. The Government should introduce compulsory 'return to business/industry' refresher weeks for all vocational lecturers.

102. The Government's Corporate Social Responsibility (CSR) agenda – which we say something about later – should be expanded to cover employers encouraging their employees to take an active part in skills training either by being assessors and or becoming visiting lecturers/trainers in colleges.

103. The Government, working with the AoC, should also consider new incentives to those in employment to become vocational tutors and assessors and visiting lecturers. And the Government should ensure that the new qualifications requirement on all college lecturers is not placing too many barriers in the way of vocational specialists entering teaching. The qualification framework should be reviewed, with Lifelong Learning UK (LLUK) and representatives of colleges, and a new category of vocational tutor should be developed.

104. Wider workforce issues are returned to later.

Tackling poor provision

105. Poor provision is concentrated in a significant minority of FE colleges. Though the number of colleges which are judged inadequate is falling the position is still unacceptable. The Government cannot allow this position to continue.

106. The situation must be addressed as it has a negative impact on learners and debilitates and dents confidence in FE colleges. The Review heard concerns about whether there are adequate mechanisms in the current system to deal with colleges judged to be failing. Time should be called on those institutions that have relentlessly failed their learning communities. Putting such institutions on a 'fresh start' would address the poor service they deliver and the impact this has on the image of the college system as a whole. Effective inspection and improvement work is essential to the self-esteem of FE colleges.

107. The LSC should take responsibility for developing an intensive development programme, in consultation with colleges and others, for tackling under-performing colleges who are in the inadequate category.

108. Using the benchmarks mentioned earlier, colleges that do not meet the grade should be subject to a notice to improve which will last for one year. The QIA and CEL should work with the LSC and the colleges to give major support to these institutions during this period. If this development work does not lead to the necessary improvements, those colleges or departments that do not pass a re-inspection should be made the subject

of a contestability review, organised by the LSC which could lead to:

- another college or provider taking over responsibility for a department or specific area of provision;

- another college or provider taking over the management of the college for at least five years; or

- closure of the college, with assets and provision responsibilities being reallocated within the area.

109. This would be a major driver for improving quality. In the short term this focus should rightly be on failing colleges. However, attention should increasingly be on moving satisfactory provision to good and then from good to excellent. No learner or employer should feel that they have to accept provision which is merely satisfactory. Everyone should want weak providers and weak provision to be addressed vigorously and no-one should condone coasting providers that are not striving for excellence. The short term focus should rightly be on failing providers. However, attention should increasingly be on provision where there is clearly room for improvement.

The Quality Improvement Landscape

110. The world of FE college oversight is crowded. There is a galaxy of oversight, inspection and accreditation bodies [BOX 4].They need to be rationalised, co-ordinated and focused. The burden of inspection of FE colleges would be lightened if only one inspecting body held responsibility. It is suggested later that the Adult Learning Inspectorate (ALI) and Ofsted should be merged and a single inspectorate should cover post-16 provision.

BOX 4

List of organisations with a monitoring/inspection/improvement role in FE colleges

Inspectorates

Ofsted

The Adult Learning Inspectorate

The Quality Assurance Agency (for HE in FE)

Funding/Monitoring/planning influence

The Learning and Skills Council

The Higher Education Funding Council for England

Job Centre Plus

Local Authorities

Regional Development Agencies

Sector Skills Councils

Improvement /Standards Setting

The Standards Unit (DfES)

Local Learning and Skills Councils

The Learning and Skills Development Agency / Quality Improvement Agency

The Centre for Excellence in Leadership

Lifelong Learning UK

Institute for Learning

The Qualifications and Curriculum Authority

Awarding Bodies

111. The Standards Unit, within the DfES, has filled a solid role in recent years working on quality, standards and workforce issues. The establishment of the unit within the DfES was a reflection that the Department felt it was important to have an external group stimulating and challenging teachers and trainers across the network. The argument in this report is that the system needs to be simplified and clarified as lines of accountability are confused, with several bodies involved. We therefore recommend that the plan to relocate the Standards Unit's resources to the QIA and to other organisations should be expedited. This is consistent with the prime advisory responsibility for quality improvement strategies that rests with the QIA and the executive responsibility that rests with FE colleges and the LSC.

WE RECOMMEND

We therefore recommend a determined drive to improve quality in all FE colleges. In particular we recommend that:

- The LSC should, working with FE colleges, develop an intensive one year development programme for the under-performing colleges who are in the failing category. The QIA and CEL should give major support to these institutions during this period. Those colleges or departments that do not pass a re-inspection should be made the subject of a contestability review, organised by the LSC, which could result in the removal of services, changes in management or the closure of the college.

- The QIA and the LSC should develop a new self-assessment model for FE colleges as a foundation for movement towards to self-regulation. It should be based upon a broader set of measures of success and indicators of impact, and a set of benchmarks including value for money.

- As many of the ideas come directly from staff working in FE colleges, the QIA should consult widely on a national quality improvement strategy and then publish it as a firm framework for implementation by colleges.

- The Government should further rationalise the oversight, inspection and accreditation bodies.

- The Government should expedite plans to relocate Standards Unit resources with the QIA.

- The Government should introduce compulsory return to business/industry refresher weeks for all vocational lecturers.

- The Government's CSR agenda should be expanded to cover employers encouraging their employees to take an active part in skills training either by being assessors and or becoming visiting lecturers/trainers in colleges.

- The Government should consider a new policy for giving incentives to those in employment to become vocational tutors and visiting lecturers.

- The Government and the QIA should ensure long-term continuous improvements in teaching and learning by extending the national teaching and learning change programme to cover other key areas.

- The Government should ensure that the new qualifications requirement on all college lecturers is not placing too many barriers in the way of vocational specialists entering teaching. The qualification framework should be reviewed and a new category of vocational tutor should be developed.

- The Government should consider undertaking value for money studies, including asset utilisation, and bringing forward proposals for efficiencies in procurement.

SECTION 3.3: THE LEARNER IMPERATIVE

What learners say

112. What learners and learner representatives have said about their experience of FE colleges has been central to the Review. Learners have told us of their very positive experiences of FE colleges:

- Younger learners have been attracted by the range of choice of subjects and qualifications in colleges, including the ability to mix academic and vocational learning and by the more adult environment compared to schools. Many younger learners view college as a place for 'growing up' and developing the skills and experiences that will prepare them for employment opportunities.

Considering I didn't get any GCSEs at school or any qualifications, it's really important. It's really going to help me find a job later.

Young male studying full time

- Adult learners made very powerful comments about life changing positive learning experiences in FE colleges.

- The overall experience of FE colleges by learners with learning difficulties and /or disabilities is extremely positive, with learners enjoying greater social inclusion than previously experienced in other learning environments.

I actually wrote a book about 18 months ago using the voice-activated computer system and some of the knowledge that I've learned on the ECDL and RSA Word-Processing 2... So yes, really good and good that I could still do it even after having got a disability.

Adult female studying part time

113. Our work with learners has shown that FE colleges have an invaluable asset in the good will and commitment of learners.

It's a nice feeling to have studied, done what we want to do, achieved your course, got your certificates and you really feel proud of your achievements

Adult female studying full time

114. But the news is not all good. As we mentioned earlier, whilst national success rates have increased significantly over the past 5 years, these averages conceal huge variations by college and curriculum area. In some areas, particularly 16-18 year olds on long vocational courses, retention rates are still too low. Learners are – for a range of reasons – dropping out of courses early. This is often a wasted

“ *Somewhere where I can learn further on from school; somewhere where it's more grown up and to prepare me for a job* ”

Young male studying full time

“ *It [going to college] changed my life.* ”

Adult female studying part time

“ *It's made me go further within the company because I've taken this course on...* ”

Adult male studying full time

> *" A lot of education now, in FE, is geared at the 16-25 age group and not about lifelong learning "*

Adult female studying part time

> *" Initially it was to gain further qualifications to aid job search and job promotion, but as I've got older jobs are more difficult to find... Sometimes it's like chasing the Holy Grail "*

Adult male studying full time

opportunity for the individual, and clearly not good value for money.

115. We heard comments from adults about the college environment being more suited to traditional methods of educating younger people.

116. And younger learners complain of an excessive focus on exams and assessment and of the lack of time to make use of informal learning opportunities.

117. From interviews with 100 current and former learners, we found that there is a huge diversity of meaning that learners attach to their experience in FE colleges. For the majority, the experience of FE represents an opportunity to achieve. Learners attach very different significance to achievement and for some, qualifications are considered an attractive measure of achievement. For other learners, achievement is measured by the outcomes they expect to achieve (skills, knowledge, experience, self confidence) and the steps these outcomes make possible is of much greater significance (new employment, education and life opportunities).

118. A primary focus on skills development will count for little if those who learn in the FE environment are disappointed and emerge unfulfilled, with potential un-met and few, if any, new opportunities. We need to ensure learning programmes maximise access, retention and achievement and ensure learners develop the knowledge, skills and competencies that will enable them to access employment opportunities or progress to higher levels of learning and skills.

> *I thought it would be more mind expanding than it was, really. I think you have to go to university for that. I don't know, maybe not, but the subjects that I took didn't seem to really challenge me as much as I think they should have done*

Adult male studying part time

LEARNER NEEDS

Collective commitment

119. The learner interviews revealed that being part of a group with a collective commitment to learning is very important to learners. From the learner's perspective, the challenge for FE colleges is to build and sustain the collective commitment to learning by providing engaging learning experiences that are relevant, hands-on and interactive, and allow them to progress on to other learning or a job.

Accessibility and flexibility

120. Commitment to learning is strongly linked to accessibility and the flexibility of the offer. This includes:

- facilities and resources to support the needs of learners such as crèche facilities, travel arrangements and financial support.

- providing learning that is personalised to the learner's needs, and at a time, and in a place which is convenient.

- addressing emotional barriers to entry to the learning community, such as lack of social confidence.

- challenging mistrust and prejudice between learners.

My ideal college would be something warm and welcoming, that people would want to attend with pleasant, friendly staff and tutors... Some place where people would want to be amongst friends while they are learning.

Adult female studying part time

121. As part of their development of a stronger skills focus, colleges, especially GFECs, need to be open for business all year round and allow new learners to start at any time of the year. FE colleges also need to make more of their provision available in community venues outside the college. Although many colleges are moving towards more flexible delivery offers (especially for bespoke employer provision) the perception remains that college are mainly term-time institutions. FE colleges should examine their offer for employers and adult learners to see how far it is a year round offer. They should also proactively examine the perceptions about the flexibility of delivery amongst employers and the local community to see what actions need to be taken to make the skills focus truly flexible.

Un-committed learners

122. Colleges also need to do more to manage the impact of uncommitted learners. Whilst learners are very tolerant of the different needs and perspectives of other learners they are very intolerant of the lack of commitment by others. Learners also look to a demonstration of commitment to a successful experience at college from the staff and the college as a whole. The clearest expression of such commitment is the environment and ethos of the FE

college. Learners look for environments that demonstrate a commitment to their health and well-being, support the development of a learning community and celebrate and show confidence in their achievements.

Better navigation

123. Consistently, learners report that information advice and guidance is out of date, fragmented and ill informed.

124. Current 'navigational aids' include the Connexions Service for young people, the national **learndirect** online and telephone service for adults, and local next step services which are designed to offer face to face information and advice; and colleges themselves provide a range of support at each stage of the learner's journey, from pre-entry to help with progression opportunities and job seeking.

125. But there is considerable local variation and scope for incoherence across ages and providers. Services for adults are a long way from giving everyone advice and guidance when and where they need it. There is also a perception – fair or otherwise – that advice is sometimes prejudiced in favour of universities and non-college provision.

126. We believe that the provision of learner-focused advice and guidance is a key area for action: networks of pathways are not much use without signposts. Major changes are planned through the Youth Matters Green Paper proposals, published in July 2005, which would see responsibility for funding information, advice and guidance for young people devolved from the Connexions Services to local authorities, working through children's trusts,

> *They had crèche facilities... and it was a lot less expensive than going to a private nursery. They offered [my daughter a place] straightaway, and it's right next to the college too...... maybe more places in the crèche, because I know a couple of people couldn't actually get a place.*

Adult female studying full time and part time courses

> " *I would have like to be in the Students Union, but at the time it just seemed like such a popularity contest!* "

Young female studying full time

colleges and schools. The Government also has plans within the Skills Strategy for reforming information, advice and guidance services for adults and these provide a good basis for taking this forward. We think that urgent action is needed to improve the services to young people and adults. As a matter of principle, the Government should ensure that the different systems and information sources that exist to help people navigate learner pathways are made more learner-focused, understandable and accessible to improve choice.

127. Local provider networks (which we say more about in section 4.1) should be required to collaborate in describing and communicating their services and helping people to find their way around. And it is essential that the information provided by colleges and others to external agencies on their current provision is up to date. This includes information provided to the national telephone helpline and online service – **learndirect**. As a condition of receiving public funding, providers should also be under an obligation to keep the information for these external signposting services current and helpful to potential learners.

National Institute of Adult Continuing Education (NIACE): Committee of Inquiry into Adult Learners in Further Education

128. The recent NIACE Committee of Inquiry has also looked at learner needs. It identifies important new demands on FE colleges with an ageing population and a rise in civic engagement. Education and training systems must not only meet the needs of people as they are, but who they

might become. NIACE also suggest that successful engagement in learning by adults is restricted by current public support arrangements. The quality and focus of learner and learning support services are also critical. Current structures and policies do not meet the needs of many adult learners who require flexible patterns of delivery, including outreach courses in the community to fit learning alongside other demands in their lives. Similarly, employers seek flexible provision that does not sit comfortably with conventional educational structures.

Listening to learners

129. FE colleges and stakeholders need to systematically listen to learners. Learner involvement and representation at local and national level is key to improved performance by colleges and improved outcomes for learners. Learner representation is under-developed in the FE college system and there has been little research to monitor the extent to which learner representatives represent the student population. There is also little evidence to measure the impact of learner representatives in their attempt to voice the views of their peers.

In terms of directing the class (as a class representative), its about finding their needs, seeing where they're going wrong, how they can be helped ... it means giving up your lunch break, attending and finding out what do they want. (Young male studying full time)

Learner surveys

130. There is also no statutory requirement for FE colleges to conduct learner satisfaction surveys. Although most colleges do carry out such surveys and are encouraged to use the LSC national learning survey template, they are free to design their own surveys, leading to an inconsistent picture.

131. FE colleges should be required to collect learners' views in a consistent and systematic way as a key way of improving college provision. And they should consult learners on any major changes to their learning and learning environment.

132. We think that there needs to be a consistent and systematic way of gathering learner views at the local level to improve college provision and also to inform the planning arrangements and patterns for provision for an area. This will be a vital element of any longer term more towards greater self regulation and a key element of a college learning entitlement. And it is increasingly important to give learners a stronger voice, if we are expecting them to pay for that learning. Learners will want to consider the opportunity cost of studying and will demand a more personalised, excellent service in return. Lessons can be learnt from the Danish model where the learner voice is a central part of self assessment [BOX 5].

133. The results of learner surveys should be published locally in a learner report and aggregated and published nationally. They should also form the basis of a discussion, at least once a year, by the college's board of governors and should lead to fresh action to focus services on learner needs.

Colleges will not have problems encouraging students to enrol and maintain their education if discussions of our sort are done regularly and assessed effectively

evaluation comment from a learner participating in one of the learner workshops.

134. The learners' report will reflect the validity of the focus on skills and the quality of work done to develop these skills. It is a cross-cutting issue, but very close to the heart of the quest for improved quality. The additional challenge is to equip college staff with the skills to engage in and act on learner feedback and avoid consultation becoming an unhelpful 'wish list' activity.

LSC learner panel

135. We also think the LSC needs a better way of understanding learners and potential learners views. We recommend that the LSC should set up learner panels which include representatives of local learners and the wider community (to capture the needs of potential learners). The interviews we held with the 100 learners led to a series of questions [BOX 6]. The local and national learner panels should discuss these questions and consider what action should be taken locally as a result.

BOX 5

Listening to Learners in Denmark

The 'learner voice' is an important aspect of the quality assurance process and the design of vocational education. Learners are able to influence both their own training and the overall learning environment. This is done by involving learners in the planning of the teaching and training via student councils and student representation on the Board of Directors where learners have the opportunity to voice their views.

There is a legal requirement to conduct annual learner surveys and post the results on their website. And this information is scrutinised by the Ministry who will take action if performance is judged to be poor.

BOX 6

Examples of questions about learners' needs from the interviews with 100 learners

Can measures of success be developed that more accurately reflect achievements as learners understand them, and what place should they have alongside qualifications?

If there is a tension between providing skills and the broader range of achievements sought by learners, how can FE colleges best handle this in serving their local communities?

How can colleges and government ensure that action on diversity is understood to be a critical lever for improving the learning experience of all learners and not just a measure to improve access for a few?

What is the role of colleges in rehabilitating the most marginalised and alienated members of society? How much negative impact on the learning experiences of others, and of what kind, can be tolerated?

Training for Learner Representatives

136. We recommend also that there is more training for learner representatives in colleges to ensure they are equipped to participate effectively. College managers need to commit the necessary time and resources to allowing that training to take place. And they need to consult with learners about the form of the training and who caries it out.

WE RECOMMEND

Much of what we say throughout this report about improving the focus, quality and local collaboration will make a huge difference to the learner experience, but specifically in this area we recommend that:

- FE colleges should be required to collect learners' views in a consistent and systematic way as a key way of improving college provision. FE colleges should be required to publish this information annually in a learner report, together with their plans for addressing the issues. The LSC should aggregate this nationally and publish it.

- FE colleges should also consult learners on major issues impacting on their learning environment. This should be part of a college learning entitlement.

- The Government should expedite its reforms of information, advice and guidance to improve services to learners.

- The Government and LSC should introduce a requirement on providers to provide an objective shared service to help learners find appropriate courses (part of their requirement to collaborate).

- The LSC should establish local and national learner panels to provide a stronger learner voice in determining local needs.

- The Government should ensure that there is more training for learner representatives in colleges to ensure they are equipped to participate effectively.

SECTION 3.4: THE EMPLOYER IMPERATIVE

137. Despite many good local examples, the relationship between employers and FE colleges is patchy and needs to be significantly improved. Employers have repeatedly said that FE colleges are not meeting their needs. According to the LSC National Employers Skills Survey (2004), only 15% of employers make use of FE colleges when seeking solutions to their training and skills needs. Research by DfES in 2003 found that 90% of college principals believe that over the next three to five years their institutions will need to become more responsive to the needs of employers.

138. We anticipate that Sandy Leitch will have a wide range of comments and analysis that will speak to the skill needs of employers, when he reports. In the meantime there are some issues which stand out. Whilst FE colleges need to become more responsive to employers many employers need to think more systematically about their medium term skills needs, develop business cases concerning them and discuss these with FE colleges and other providers. In North Carolina [BOX 7], colleges are very responsive to employer skill needs.

Changing employment patterns

139. The setting for employer engagement is complex. In the days when the UK economy was structured around a small number of large industries in particular localities, FE colleges in those localities could mould their provision around the limited requirements of the local industrial base. But local economies have changed. Few localities are dependent on single industries; most have diversified. Consequently, FE colleges have a less clear local economic profile to guide course provision. And employers rightly expect a different level of service and want training to be in the workplace and/or at a convenient time. Moreover, it is far harder to maintain a fertile conversation with a diverse local economy of small businesses than with an economy dominated by a few strategic businesses. Not surprisingly, college/employer dialogue has become less satisfactory.

Other local providers

140. Although FE colleges have an important role to play in developing vocational skills, they are not the exclusive player. Independent providers already provide over 200,000 apprenticeships and won a significant part of the business available through the ETPs. Many private providers offer a wide range of off the shelf and bespoke training packages for employers. And universities also provide strong elements of training for the workplace as well as giving learners higher level skills that have workplace

---

BOX 7

North Carolina

In North Carolina the 58 colleges are the arm of economic development. 'Community' in this state means business community and colleges are integral to economic success, often taking over, or replacing, in-company training departments. The colleges are one-stop-shops for businesses to get training, business advice, problem solving and infrastructural funding.

The North Carolina view is that community education is about occupational development to further the economic development of the State. The colleges create an employment pool for companies and High Schools are being developed on college campuses to integrate into company needs at an earlier stage. Speed of response is vital to companies and only colleges that can achieve very fast response to company needs do well.

Throughout America, the local Chambers of Commerce have a close strategic alliance with their trusted community college sector. The Chief Executive to Chief Executive relationships are vital between companies and college presidents. Community Colleges sometimes work with individual companies to develop special projects e.g. getting young people who have no role models into a successful work ethos.

The 'public value' of a Community College is carefully assessed and in North Carolina this is inextricably linked to workforce development.

This clear focus on the economy and employability and close relationships with local businesses and chambers of commerce enable colleges in North Carolina to respond effectively and quickly to employer skill needs.

---

relevance. Colleges should be able to compete for employer business, but on the basis of quality in an open contestable market. Many colleges already do this (see Leicester College box). Improving quality and choice for employers is vital and the plans set out in the Skills White Paper to develop the National Employer Training Programme (NETP) is an important way to develop a more demand-led system for adult training.

CoVEs and Skills Academies

141. As we said earlier, the creation of a network of over 300 CoVEs in colleges and other providers has helped raise the profile and reputation of FE colleges. And the development of the new sector based Skills Academies provide a further opportunity, providing leadership to CoVEs and to sectoral

BOX 8

Leicester College

The College has developed its own unique commercial operation, S4B (Skills for Business) to deliver the Employer Training Pilot. This offers a one-stop shop for employers to access training with funding to Level 2. Its role is to manage initial meetings with the LSC and employers, co-ordinate the College's response within curriculum areas and establish and maintain systems to monitor performance, invoice for funding and report back to the LSC. The College received £78,000 pump priming from the local LSC to develop the infrastructure for the service which was based on an earlier proposal in the College's Workforce Development Strategy. It now employs five Training Consultants who act as account managers for the pilot and all other employer focussed provision. They have relationships with specific curriculum areas or sector specialisms and work closely with their respective curriculum area, or across relevant areas in the case of those with sector specialisms. This enables curriculum staff to focus on delivering provision and on ensuring that the provision is tailored to the employers' needs. The College delivered around 1,200 learners and an income of around £800,000 in 2004/05 and is one of the largest NETP providers in the area. The College delivers training to employers when and where they want it.

BOX 9

Warwickshire College

Trident Technology and Business Centre

Warwickshire College, through its pathfinder CoVE status in General Engineering, invested £10 million in a new Technology and Business Centre. The facility is at the heart of attracting inward investment to the area and supplying appropriate skills for companies.

The centre is focussed on skills development and is an up to date, high class skills-based training facility, attractive to local industry and the business community. The Trident Centre provides an environment that supports growth in local and regional industry. The Centre also provided valuable opportunities for school children to experience modern business and technology practices in a state of the art environment.

provision in FE colleges. Improving productivity in the workforce requires provision tailored to the particular needs of the business in question. FE colleges should have the opportunity to become increasingly involved in this provision, but after a competitive process where they can demonstrate that they offer the best option locally [BOX 8].

Regional and national infrastructure

142. Many local employers do not become closely involved with their local colleges. The link between skilling people to enter the workforce and the individual recruitment and training activity of individual firms is often too remote for many employers to justify active engagement with the college. But there is a profound economic and regional interest in ensuring that localities have a viable pool of employable labour. Therefore, the most important levels for the education/economy dialogue are at a level beyond the individual college.

143. The infrastructure arrangements that the Government has put in place through the Skills Strategy, including SSCs, Sector Skills Agreements and Regional Skills Partnerships, should ensure that the strategy for supply of skills, training, business support and labour market services is planned, managed and delivered in a coherent, collaborative way which reflects the priorities set out by Regional Development Agencies (RDAs) and in Regional Economic Strategies. And many colleges have good relationships with local economic development units in local authorities. The mechanisms are there for lateral integration of sectoral and regional needs but it is too early to evaluate their effectiveness. However, we recommend that these mechanisms and their effectiveness will need to be reviewed by the Government when it receives the recommendations of the Leitch Review of Skills next year.

Local responsiveness

144. There is no one-size-fits-all model of successful employer involvement and responsiveness. The Review heard of lots of local initiatives. There is also plenty of research into effective employer responsiveness, including the recent work done by LSDA and by Ofsted. And there are some impressive regional initiatives, including the Action for Business Colleges model developed in the South East. And we saw examples of how, in the US, Community Colleges are a key part of their business community [BOX 7, page 35]. The LSC's proposals in *agenda for change* to create a nationwide network of quality marked colleges and other providers which are focused on the needs of employers and the workforce

are a further step in the right direction. There is scope for greater creativity in partnership working with employers and in harnessing their views and expertise. We recommend local or regional Work or Skills Boards of senior employers are established to help Regional Skills Partnerships.

145. FE Colleges can also strengthen their links with employers through the enterprise agenda, working closely with schools and universities who are also promoting enterprise in education. Practical suggestions include getting students to take enterprise projects, engaging entrepreneurs as practitioner lecturers, and establishing entrepreneur clubs for their students [BOXES 9 & 10].

Trade Unions

146. The Review was also impressed with the powerful role trade unions have developed in promoting training in the workplace. We saw how unions play a key role in the Danish system [BOX 11]. The Trades Union Congress (TUC) led Union Academy is a welcome development and, working with local colleges, will help more people take up learning opportunities in the workplace.

147 We believe the establishment of this academy is an excellent way of developing effective skills support networks to help unions engage in skills development at local, regional and national level, often working through their local college. It is another good example of the hub and spoke model, which we believe essential to improve how good practice is identified and disseminate. Its key role in further developing union learning representatives (ULRs) will be vital. We heard how ULRs are making a big difference in raising demand for

learning in many areas, especially amongst workers with lower skill levels. Over 12,000 ULRs have been trained to date.

BOX 10

Remploy

Remploy Derby – The learning centre at the site is now run as a satellite unit for the college, by the college. Currently courses are offered internally for Remploy employees, but plans are now in place to extend the offer to;

- Friends & family

- Other local people with learning difficulties and disabilities people – via Remploy Interwork

- Employees of other businesses local to the site

Derby college have invested almost £50,000 worth of IT equipment to help set up the centre

Remploy St Helens – Have had a strong relationship for several years now. On the back of that relationship and a proven track record, the site and college were able to jointly gain funding for 10 PCs to be installed into the new learning centre. Further, because of the business need at the St Helens site, the college specifically gained accreditation from the awarding body for the pharmaceutical industry and gained funding to provide NVQs at levels 1 and 2 specifically for the business.

Remploy Mansfield – The site has a significant number of employees who either live with elderly parents or live in sheltered accommodation. Following discussion with West Notts College, the site set up a kitchen area. The college now deliver literacy training through the medium of teaching employees to prepare and cook food and undertake domestic chores such as washing clothes.

BOX 11

Role of Trade Unions in Denmark

In Denmark, social partners (which include Trade Unions and Trade Committees) have a central role in the design and development of vocational education and in all stages of quality assurance. They ensure that vocational programmes match the needs and demands of employers and the labour market at both national and regional level. College boards are made up of equal numbers of social partners plus learners.

The systematic involvement of social partners enables colleges to keep abreast of company skill needs and workforce development issues

- The Government and the LSC should consider what further action should be taken to improve engagement between colleges and employers when it receives the advice of the Leitch Review of Skills next year.

- In the meantime, colleges should look at what more they need to do to improve their offer to employers both in terms of the pool of employability and skills, and in their response to specific employer needs.

- And employers need to think more systematically about their medium term skills needs and discuss these with their local college or other provider.

- Consideration is given to establishing local or regional Work and Skills Boards of senior employers to help Regional Skills Partnerships and providers identify gaps in future demand and supply of skills.

- The Government and the LSC should continue with its programme of reforms including the Skills Strategy and the LSC's *agenda for change*, but these should be reviewed in the light of the Leitch recommendations.

- The Government should continue to support union initiatives to improve skills development including the new Union Academy and ULRs.

SECTION 3.5:
THE REPUTATION IMPERATIVE

148. FE colleges should be enjoying a golden age, given the correspondence between its potential and the nation's needs. Colleges have an important role to play in delivering key Government priorities and strategies yet they are hampered by their reputation and profile, compared to schools and universities.

Improving awareness and credibility

149. There are two important aspects to reputation. The first is about how clearly you and others understand what you are there to do. The second is about how well you are seen to be doing it. But success in performance terms is of doubtful value if the wrong objectives are being pursued, and this reinforces the importance of shared clarity about purpose.

150. Whilst FE colleges have done a significant amount in recent years to promote their successes, including improvements in educational achievement, our evidence suggests they are still not sufficiently well understood and valued. For too many people, particularly employers (we have found) the experience is that colleges are not delivering what is needed. This view leads to (and then reflects, in a negative cycle) a lack of positive engagement. Old and inappropriate buildings, out of date equipment and technology and sometimes a lack of up to date knowledge and experience amongst staff, all help to create the feeling of a network which is struggling to find and keep its place.

151. Nationally, and locally, where colleges should be recognised as important institutions contributing to economic development and social cohesion, they are not always seen as dynamic learning environments. In her report on Widening Participation in Further Education (1997), Helena Kennedy reported 'appalling ignorance among decision makers and opinion formers' about what goes on in colleges. This is still largely the case today.

152. The diversity of college activity, often seen as a strength, brings confusion about their role and purpose. Their very responsiveness to the different agendas set by Government creates a fuzzy and confused image. The Review heard many different perceptions of what colleges do. We also heard a lot about the lack of a 'FE college' brand not being helped by the plethora of qualifications and the fact that many schools and universities are also called colleges. The divergent demands placed on them weaken their voice and standing with national decision makers.

153. Without clarity of purpose colleges will always struggle to build a positive reputation and attract support and resources. Even with this greater clarity there will remain a key task of building understanding, confidence and reputation. A way must be found of saying who colleges are and what they do that is clear and simple and identifies their distinctive role.

154. But there is good news too. The results of a public perceptions survey, undertaken for the Review by MORI, are given below. It found 60% of respondents felt knowledgeable about

FE colleges, and those that have used a college were positive about the difference it made [BOX 12].

The need for change

155. Good repute stands with clarity of purpose and quality of service as key things that change should seek to achieve. The responsibility of promoting a positive purpose and reputation rests partly with national politicians and national managers who need to promote and convey clarity; but there is a vital need also for FE college principals to project a positive vision of their service to society, particularly at the local level.

156. Our conversations with the American Association of Community Colleges (AACC) in the USA, suggest that their improved standing had been achieved over a period by:

- Emphasising their key virtues such as open access, economic responsiveness, academic progression in a simple manner;

- Consistently using articulate community college presidents, employers and students as their advocate;

- Demonstrating how quickly and constructively they can respond to local economic need;

- Having a small team working in Washington positively advocating the case for colleges.

157. We advocate a quick review of reputation led by DfES, involving LSC and AoC to come forward with a range of practical proposals that capitalise on this lead. This review could result in a greater involvement of principals in national representation, in particular

BOX 12

Public Perceptions of FE – Research carried out by MORI for the review (2005)

- The majority of respondents felt knowledgeable about FE colleges. However, two in five knew only a little, not very much or nothing at all, with older respondents aged 35-50 least likely to feel knowledgeable.

- The public view the main role of FE colleges as the provision of learning opportunities for young people to equip them for work.

- The delivery of vocational training and providing young people with a route to university or higher education are also perceived to be key functions of FE colleges.

- One in ten say they do not know what the role of FE colleges is, but this figure increases to 16% for those with no personal experience of FE.

- The majority think that FE colleges fulfil their role well, with opinions most positive when asked about FE colleges in general rather than local colleges themselves.

- The vast majority of people who have used an FE college would recommend it to others, largely because they found it useful for getting a job or improved how they did their job.

- Among the very small minority of people who said they would not recommend FE, the main reason cited was the quality of the teaching and training.

- The main barrier to FE for respondents is lack of time, which is principally the case for those working full-time and with more than two children in the household.

- Other key barriers include family/ childcare commitments, work pressures and affordability of courses.

those from larger, successful colleges where management capacity and capability exists to release them for this work. There is a strong need for articulate FE college principals to be explaining the services they give to society and how colleges can make a significant contribution to the economy and to developing fulfilled citizens.

WE RECOMMEND

- The Government and the LSC should promote widely the clear purpose and strong brand for FE linked to the skills mission and there needs to be a long term consistency in this promotion.

- All college principals should be active locally in promoting their services and the college brand and vision to local stakeholders. Principals of the larger FE colleges, in particular, should take on a promotional role at regional and national level.

- The DfES, LSC and AoC should be invited to bring forward proposals for reputation management.

At the heart of these proposals is the need to simplify and explain how society will benefit. It will also be important that staff working in colleges seek to leave behind the concerns of the past and move to project the potential benefit they bring for society.

Part 4
IMPROVING MANAGEMENT AND FUNDING

SECTION 4.1: LOCAL PROVISION

158. This section is about arrangements for the provision of learning services at the local level – the supply side – rather than how decisions are made about what should be provided (the demand side is dealt with in the next main section).

159. It may be helpful to say that no 'big bang', structural reconfiguration of FE college provision is envisaged. Too many big public service structural changes take a long time to implement, cost a great deal and can alienate the very key workers on whom the system depends.

160. Three things are needed: first, improved relationships and coordination of what is there; secondly, better public information about it;

and thirdly, a gradual evolution of provision to be better matched to need, including opening up the market to new provision. This stands much more chance of effectiveness and acceptance.

Learning pathways and managed provider networks

'Students need clear pathways. Not everyone wakes up at the age of 12 and decides to become a dentist, and then proceeds through the system. It is important to let qualified students move between institutions'

Bob Rae – Ontario: A leader in Learning

161. The needs of learners change over time and most learners wish to advance on a number of fronts. Sometimes it will be possible to meet

an individual's needs, over time, in one FE college setting but often it will not. As we mentioned earlier in this report, a skills focus should lead to the development across colleges of specialisms connected through hub and spoke arrangements, regionally and nationally. And a properly learner-focused system is likely to have a range of different components. Not all of these will be institution-based; not all will be strictly local; not all will be provided by the public sector. But the components must be integrated in two senses: they are part of a single system of local provision and they can be accessed easily along 'learner pathways'.

162. In order to achieve a genuinely user-responsive system, learners, and those who will employ them, will be best served by a coordinated, pluralist

BOX 13

The S7 Consortium of Surrey Sixth Form Colleges
(Esher/Farnham/Godalming/Reigate/
Spelthorne/Strode's/Woking)

S7 is a consortium of Sixth Form Colleges in Surrey. The S7 Colleges successfully meet the needs of thousands of young people aged 14 to 19 and many adults in the Surrey area.

In an increasingly competitive and ever-changing educational environment, their aim is to work together to promote the abiding benefits of Sixth Form College education and to develop the quality of their provision.

The seven Surrey Sixth Form Colleges have developed a consortium to organise joint training for Newly Qualified Teachers, a leadership programme for middle managers, and subject networks and conferences for tutors working in the colleges. This provision is specifically designed and developed by members to improve teaching and learning and improve quality across the colleges.

network of provision that is flexible, comprehensive and transparent. The implication of this is that across a local area a range of different providers will need to work together locally, including independent providers. In some cases, certainly, many facilities will in fact be provided from a single base, and it may be appropriate then to conceive of a network with a strong centre – but a network still.

163. But if that flexibility is not to exacerbate current levels of confusion, the system must also be coordinated, comprehensive and transparent. Indeed, coordination will be key especially for the delivery of an effective 14-19 phase. As the Working Group on 14-19 reform proposed, all young people in all areas should be entitled to access the full range of learning options. And the Government has translated this into a learning entitlement for all 14 lines of the specialised diploma and a single local prospectus. This cannot be achieved without a significant level of collaboration between providers including the sharing of buildings and resources. But there must also be significant collaboration between the local authority and the local LSC, with absolute clarity at local level of roles and responsibilities. The proposals in the Schools White Paper for a new role for local authorities as a local commissioner and champion of parents and pupils will significantly help.

Managed provider networks

164. We believe what is needed are *managed provider networks*. This means providers managing network activity together, as well as their

own services independently. They should have the freedom to devise the best arrangements to achieve the desired results. But they also need to be responsive to broader local and regional priorities within a planning framework established by the local LSC. This is about getting the right balance between the strategic responsibilities of the local commissioner, and the important responsibilities of colleges and their corporations for deciding how local needs should be met.

165. We prefer the concept of 'provider network' to 'alliance' (which implies unity against a common enemy) or 'confederation' (which is too grand and institutional). 'Consortium' is relevant too as a joint arrangement that a network can produce for specific purposes. 'Partnership' is a also a good word, but we reserve that for local arrangements for shaping what is provided rather than managing it (see next section). 'Network' sits comfortably alongside the idea of learner pathways.

166. The Review saw some examples of strong local networks [BOX 13] and consideration will need to be given to how other good networking practice can be identified and promulgated.

167. In relation to 14-19, we heard concerns about the funding and governance issues associated with collaboration. Many 14-19 pathfinders are finding innovative ways around these issues. We urge the Government to ensure that options that are being tested out through these pathfinders are evaluated quickly so that these practical issues do not get in the way of further collaborative work [BOX 14].

Shared services

168. As well as working together to meet the needs of learners in a way that is easy to access, networks create opportunities for provider organisations to rationalise administrative services and use of buildings. FE colleges carry large overheads. As independent institutions, they have their own arrangements for finance, human resources, marketing, enrolment and other corporate functions. In a local setting, this is duplicative and wasteful, particularly in small or medium sized institutions. A local provider network could sponsor shared services arrangements of the kind found in other public sector areas, either hosted by one member of the confederation or supplied by an agency. There could be useful cost-reduction opportunities. The LSC in its *agenda for change* prospectus has made some initial proposals in this area which need to be developed with urgency. The LSC and the Government should provide financial incentives to local networks and to individual colleges and their governing bodies to cover the initial cost of forming provider networks for sharing services.

Best practice and innovation

169. The Review has heard frequent statements about the patchiness of provision. We need to bring all providers up to the level of the best. As well as the quality and inspection regimes discussed elsewhere, the spread of best practice and innovation will help towards that end. Managed provider networks will create a forum for sharing new ideas and best practice on a newly collaborative rather than competitive basis.

Better information

170. As we proposed in the Learner Imperative section (section 3.3), an important role for local provider networks is the provision of up to date information and advice. This is vital to help learners navigate the system. For 14-19, the proposed local prospectus will give learners greater ability to choose, and put an even greater premium on quality and responsiveness. As we recommend in section 3.3, information, advice and guidance to young people and adults needs to be improved significantly and we urge this happens as a priority.

WE RECOMMEND

- The Government and the LSC ensure that the development of managed provider networks at local level is co-ordinated across the country in a systematic, rather than opportunistic way, in particular to support the Government's 14-19 plans.

- The Government should introduce a requirement on all providers to collaborate to make this happen.

- Colleges should work together, to improve learner pathways and to realise the opportunities for economies of scale, development and innovation through shared services within a network.

- The Government should provide financial incentives to local networks and to individual colleges and their governing bodies to cover the initial cost of forming provider networks for sharing services.

BOX 14

Knowsley College 14-19 Collegiate Model.

In Knowsley, schools and colleges work together to offer new choices to pupils 14-16 year olds from all Knowsley schools have access to opportunities in the new Vocational Skills Centre based at Knowsley Community College... A GCSE in engineering is being provided jointly with a local employer. And more than 1,000 Key Stage 4 students in the Borough are benefiting from a least one day of out of school provision ranging from NVQ and GCSE college provision, to a five day Key Skills 4 work-based learning programme.

This is curriculum choice in action – with schools, colleges and employers choosing to work together within a clear local framework for the benefit of all. Extended schools can add new impetus to this – extending choice and meeting the needs of both parents and pupils.

goal of self regulation, proposed in this report will strengthen the importance of the FE college corporation and give them a vital challenge to address. Their ability to articulate and respond to local community needs, within the light touch, but broader framework set by the local commissioner will be a significant and critical job.

183. However the Review was concerned about the diversity of governing bodies. More comprehensive guidance should be developed for search committees on reaching under-represented groups and this could be part of a wider Guide to Good Governance which should be developed for FE colleges, on the lines of best governance practice. It should focus on the role of governors in the new college system envisaged in this report. It could include for example a person specification and job description for the Chair, and greater clarity about the role of governors.

Local commissioning functions

184. To improve coherence and integration at local level there is a need for a light touch local commissioner who has the capability to understand and represent the needs of the local area and coordinate local providers in developing the learning pathways and improved navigation we proposed earlier. To work effectively these must be focused on the demand side, separate from provision, but must involve providers in their assessment of what is needed and should be provided.

185. We suggest that the required local commissioning functions are to:

- act as the link between the LSC at regional level and local provision.

- systematically assess local needs, engaging strongly with employers, learners and their communities.

- develop a strong understanding of the quality, range and effectiveness of provision in an area.

- shape local provision in the light of national priorities and regional and local needs.

- to work with the regional centres to ensure that demand side priorities of employers influence local provision.

- manage market entry and exit through a contestability framework.

- ensure coherence and integration locally in funding and capital arrangements.

- with providers, assist learners and employers in understanding what is available.

- facilitate local provider networking, including working with the local authority to deliver the range of local provision, and ensure all young people have reasonable access to all 14 diploma lines in a choice of learning settings – this will also include the development of the 14-19 prospectus.

186. The commissioning role we describe above for the medium term is similar to the aspiration that the LSC has for all local LSCs, recognising that currently there is some inconsistency of application. Local LSCs need to be the pivotal centre of the local community's interest, working collaboratively with local authorities, in their new local commissioner role, to deliver the 14-19 phase we mentioned earlier. This is not a significant change in responsibilities, as envisaged under the Learning and Skills Act 2000. It is about how those responsibilities are implemented and we welcome the intentions by the LSC for the local LSC to move away from a transactional, contract compliance mode to a more strategic basis of operation. The essence of the role is to achieve a sensitive understanding of what is needed locally and to facilitate the work of providers in meeting need.

187. Developing the role of local LSC non-executive members will be critical. They have a vital leadership and advocacy role (bringing in the demand-side) and provide an important challenge and support function to the executive.

188. Transforming current local arrangements in this way is a significant challenge for the LSC to deliver. We think the LSC's proposals for changing their national, regional and local operations under its *agenda for change* reforms are a step in the right direction, but what is required is a shift in perceptions, roles and culture as well as structures. It will be important that the DfES supports the LSC in implementing the necessary changes.

189. During the time horizon for this report, five to ten years, the successful recasting of local roles is critically important and should be closely monitored.

WE RECOMMEND

- The LSC ensures as part of its *agenda for change* reforms, local LSCs implement on the commissioning functions set out above.

- Provider functions and commissioning functions should be appropriately separated, conceptually and practically.

- College governance arrangements should not be changed, but the Government, with FE colleges, should take steps to improve the diversity of governing bodies. The Government should also develop a guide to good governance to underpin the new purpose and clarity roles and responsibilities.

SECTION 4.3:
THE DEPARTMENT FOR EDUCATION AND SKILLS AND GOVERNMENT – THE STRATEGIC ARCHITECT

190. There is an enormous case for training and education across the economy in particular and society in general. FE colleges do not have a monopoly of these roles and cannot find their place in isolation from other parts of the education system. Moreover, the range of potential roles for FE colleges is extensive and strategic focus is essential.

191. FE therefore needs a strong strategic lead at national level. This must flow from a pan-sectoral vision from government, translated through the LSC in its strategic and local commissioning roles.

Broad education policy

192. It is only possible to understand the proper role of FE colleges if they are considered in the context of the whole education system. Yet the Review has been surprised at the extent of policy and administrative separation between the schools, FE and HE 'sectors' at departmental level. The DfES needs to generate an integrated and coherent view across the three 'sectors', and a coordinated approach to development. In particular, learner pathways should not be bounded or hampered by interdepartmental functional divides and qualifications should not simply reflect the untidy legacy of various policy interventions over the years. Present arrangements have the potential to create duplication as well as policy dislocation.

193. The Permanent Secretary might consider leading bi-annual conferences with the director generals and the heads of agencies and other non-departmental bodies to focus on learner benefit and national interest, with an emphasis on joined-up policy and operations.

Corporate leadership

194. Currently, the FE college is the neglected 'middle child' between universities and schools. As FE colleges offer major opportunities for the economy and individual citizens, central government should bring together the policies and operations of several departments of state, ensuring coherence and synergy. A multi-billion pound public service with a quarter of a million staff, working in such nationally important territory, should enjoy the benefits of top level commitment and representation. Whilst the government believes that it has strong and clear leadership arrangements in place, it does not feel so to the staff who work in colleges; they consider that

colleges are often given second place to universities. We recommend that the government reviews the way that the corporate leadership for skills is organised with the intention of enhancing the importance of the role.

195. Within the DfES and across government, there needs to be a stronger focus and interest in colleges and what they can offer. An injection of new energy is needed at all levels to ensure that FE colleges get to play their rightful role.

196. This is an important cross government area and there needs to be a higher public profile across all government departments. Responsibility, at cross-Government level for considering FE colleges rests with the Skills Alliance and within this group's work, it will be important to ensure that they receive the attention and profile they deserve at national level.

WE RECOMMEND

- The Government gives a stronger focus and interest in FE colleges, and what they can offer.

- The Permanent Secretary consider leading bi-annual conferences with the director generals and the heads of agencies and other non-departmental bodies to focus on learner benefit and national interest, with an emphasis on joined-up policy and operations.

SECTION 4.4: THE LEARNING AND SKILLS COUNCIL

Background

197. The LSC has had a difficult first few years and has been the object of much criticism during the course of this review. For various reasons – bureaucracy, micro-management, lack of clout at local level, and so on – the LSC has been seen to be more of a brake than an accelerator.

198. The LSC has made a number of important changes to address these concerns. Its recently established new business cycle introduced much needed integration in a year-round cycle of stock-take, planning and action. And the LSC's recently published *agenda for change* addresses directly many of the criticisms historically levelled against it and sets out measures to overcome them **[BOX 16]**. These measures are most welcome, as are the organisational changes that ensue. The LSC is currently developing implementation plans and it will be important that these establish clear, detailed, time bound actions for addressing its proposals and that they are realistic in terms of resources.

Operational leadership

199. The focus of those measures is largely on operational management matters and it is proposed that there is an opportunity now to go further and take the LSC into a stronger operational leadership role. The LSC is the only national public body with an explicit and exclusive remit around learning and skills and the dedicated budget to support that.

BOX 16

Learning and Skills Council: *agenda for change*

Launched in November 2004, the LSC *agenda for change* is a transformation programme for the learning and skills sector. It is an important reflection of the LSC's commitment to engage fully with the sector and work in partnership with colleges and training providers in a spirit of openness and transparency.

Working with the sector, the LSC has looked at how best the needs of employers can be met and the workforce skills improved; how a sector fully committed to quality and delivery to the highest standards can be built; how funding methods can be changed to support priorities with the minimum of complexity; how data collection can be simplified; how the sector can achieve business excellence, how the reputation of the sector as a whole can be enhanced and how the LSC itself needs to change to deliver on this agenda.

The LSC's aim through *agenda for change* is to build a sector comprised of colleges and providers that understand the pivotal role they have to play in delivering the learning and skills necessary for greater social justice and increased economic competitiveness, that have clear missions that they pursue relentlessly, and that understand their strengths, specialisms and unique contribution to meeting Government and LSC targets and priorities.

In July 2004, The LSC published a prospectus setting out its agenda for change proposals. It is currently developing these proposals with the sector.

200. Operational leadership by the LSC means taking up the overall strategic vision and framework set by the Government and delivering it through planning, funding and performance management of the learning and skills system, including colleges. This must involve:

- Setting the tone of discourse for FE colleges, developing a language about it that no longer derives from a deficit model but from a model of innovation, skills development, social mobility and entrepreneurialism. And then spreading this discourse both at national policy level, in Whitehall and Westminster, and with employers whether small, medium or large.

- Translating the strategic framework and vision set by Government, into a set of operational strategies for reform of FE colleges which go beyond general statements about excellence, access and so on, illustrating them instead with tangible details about how lives will be better for different learner groups, what sorts of businesses will benefit and how, how the economy will prosper and the kind of providers that will prevail. These plans should derive from the skills focus proposed in this report and be supported by current evidence. In developing these plans, the LSC should consult learners and employers, and they should also involve Chairs of FE college corporations who we feel have a valuable contribution to make at national level.

- Responding in a mature and trusted way to its primary customers: learners and employers. The LSC must set an example, taking its cue from these customer groups and adapting its focus accordingly.

- Growing in authority to have tough conversations with colleges where necessary: this means going beyond technical quality and performance measures to ensure that the strategic urgency of the skills agenda is well understood and met by colleges universally.

- Supporting innovative and high performing colleges in both tangible (financial) and intangible (marketing) terms, and playing a role in transferring innovation and knowledge.

- Being *identified* with all of the above so that the LSC can mark out a stronger identity. The opportunity is there now, with the refreshment of the system as a whole, to review and make more vivid the contribution and purpose

of FE colleges to learners and the economy.

The regional level

201. All the above requires renewed strength for the LSC and its recent changes to do just that are welcome. We have described earlier what we think its role should be at local level.

202. Establishing regional centres enables the LSC to take a wider perspective over learner needs and specialist provision to meet skills needs. Moreover, operating at the regional level enables the LSC to operate coterminously with key economic stakeholders (the Regional Development Agencies (RDAs), Regional Skills Partnerships etc). It is recommended that the LSC continues to develop its regional centres.

203. The LSC Regional Directors sitting between the national LSC office, with its close links with Government, and the locality are well placed to make this wider perspective effective in responding to regional skills priorities. As the intermediate tier, their key functions, reducing them to the essentials, would be:

- To receive and articulate strategic national aims.

- To transform them as a meaningful framework for local delivery and development.

- To link with the key regional demand side players – through the Regional Skills Partnerships – to ensure regional and sector skills priorities are fed through to local level.

- To support the production and funding of local needs based plans and ensure they support regional priorities and the needs of employers and learners.

- To manage the performance of local areas.

- To support national inspection and regulation programmes.

- To develop capacity and capability locally, including good leadership.

204. With significant activity located at regional level, there will be a need for a nationally coordinated performance management process which holds the system to account. It is proposed that there should be a yearly review by one of the scrutiny bodies which should report publicly on the effectiveness of joint working between LSC/RDA and SSCs to make sure that excellent partnerships and outcomes are being achieved. LSC at regional level needs to build strong alliances with all the relevant regional organisations and to work in partnership with them (e.g. RDAs and JobCentre Plus).

WE RECOMMEND

- The LSC should develop its operational leadership role of the system, including a key regional role between the national body and localities.

- The Government should establish a yearly review of activity at regional level and hold the system to account. (To be conducted by an independent scrutiny body).

SECTION 4.5: DFES AND THE LSC

205. The DfES has principal responsibility for determining national strategy, objectives and priorities which are then reflected in the remit assigned to the LSC. So much is obvious, but there is potential for confusion and competition at this level.

206. This review is concerned not with the relationship between the two organisations in theory, but with the practical mechanisms that will best support outcomes for employers and learners. With this in mind our view is that:

- Although DfES is responsible and accounts for the national strategy and priorities, their development will be enriched the more the Department includes in its deliberations LSC officers with useful experience of what policy works best in practice from an employer and learner perspective.

- DfES needs publicly to endorse both the new FE college 'discourse' voiced by the LSC as well as the LSC itself. It will need to stand behind LSC as the leader of the FE coalition.

- DfES must lend weight and support in both policy and political terms to the new quality regime indicated by LSC. In effect it means DfES setting out a tougher policy framework on quality for the LSC to work within.

- The DfES role is not to micro-manage LSC or FE colleges as such or replicate the LSC's role, but rather to set strategy, priorities and policy based on evidence of what produces better outcomes for employers and learners, and to hold the LSC to account. It is particularly important that the targets set by the DfES are developed in close consultation with the LSC to ensure their achievability.

- The policy focus in DfES has management implications for both organisations. Currently some DfES staff cross the line from policy into operations, leading to claims of micro-management. In effect the FE college role within DfES should be about the highest level of policy and strategy formulation, with accountability to Ministers in the context of society's needs. The LSC is not an agency of the DfES but an NDPB. It has a transformational role within its sphere of accountability.

- Equally, LSC must not micro-manage FE colleges and other providers. Crucially it must feed back to DfES relevant insights on what affects performance for the DfES to adjust policy in turn.

207. The existing formal concordat between LSC and DfES should be reviewed to ensure that lines of responsibility and the key features of the relationship are clarified as outlined above. But this is more than just about pieces of paper, it is about how the two organisations work together to achieve the required progress for learners, employers and communities. The critical feature is of trust and open communication ensuring that there is unified support for the strategy. This is a key element for success and it is vital that top management prioritise this and make sure it happens.

208. A principal recommendation of this review is that the management

overhead should be significantly reduced, particularly at the upper end of the system. Present arrangements, with approximately 460 staff in DfES working on post 16 matters, and around 4,700 staff in the LSC (though these will reduce to 3,400 under current plans), seem to us to be top heavy with the potential for duplication and the ability to make a wide range of demands on field based staff. In addition, there is significant staff resource in the inspectorate and quality improvement bodies working on post 16 issues – the Inspectorate (Ofsted and ALI) have around 500, although many on a part-time basis, QCA has around 190, CEL around 30, LLUK around 50 and LSDA 250 (this number will change with the establishment of the QIA). As we argue for the devolution of management, within lighter touch strategic frameworks, so we argue that significant resources should be devolved to the learner end of the system where they will add increased value. DfES and the LSC should continue to relocate further resources to learners.

WE RECOMMEND

- The central roles of the LSC and DfES should be refined so as to lighten the impact of centralised control and monitoring and minimise duplication and undue central demands.

- The roles of the LSC and DfES, so refined, need to be clear and complementary and this should be manifest in a relationship based on trust and openness.

- LSC and the DFES should review their formal concordat to ensure the refinement and clarification proposed above are in place.

- LSC, DfES and other organisations take further steps to ensure that significant resources are relocated to services for learners.

SECTION 4.6: FUNDING

Needs based allocation and distribution

209. It is little wonder that FE colleges feel confused and under-valued. They rejoice in the extent (and complexity) of their potential offering to learners, but find that the offer that they are able to make is influenced considerably by the funding flavour of the day. FE colleges have reacted to the mismatch between their potential to make a wide and diverse learning offer and their resources by representing disappointment over insufficient funding to government.

210. Indeed, during the course of the Review we received many representations about funding and the funding gap, and we understand these. However, we chose to take the position in our work of maximising the use of existing resources and the production of a positive and professional development plan.

The national learning model and assessment

211. Giving FE colleges a strong focus on skills will help set priorities. But to resolve the current funding impasse, there needs to be a more transparent model of need and distribution. The Treasury uses a model of the economy to assess the need for and consequences of intervention in the national economy. The national learning economy needs an equivalent strategic assessment, so that the implications of learning initiatives can be assessed for their impact on current learning needs and on the disposition of learning offers by providers. The mismatch between what FE colleges could do and what colleges should do and what colleges *can* do, funded from the public purse, leads to a delivery gap. And this gap is exacerbated by lack of clarity and understanding of the relative contributions of FE, HE and schools.

212. A national, publicly available assessment of skill needs and gaps with clear priorities, worked down to local requirements, would provide a much more transparent system for allocating resources. It would capture all the flows between the different parts of the overall education system.

213. It should inter-relate:

- Demographic change;

- The evolving national economic remit;

- Labour market intelligence;

- Locality characteristics; and

- Learning and skills pathways.

214. We believe many of the building blocks for this model exist or are planned, including at national level:

- The PSA targets which clarify funding priorities.

- Funding entitlements to fee remission for young people, those without basic skills and adults without a first full level 2 qualification.

- The National Employer Training Programme which will give employers the opportunity to access a full range of training solutions including free training for their low skilled workers.

- The Leitch Review taking a longer term view of skills needs.

- Sector Skills Councils producing their Sector Skills Agreements which will set out the actions needed to ensure the right flow of skills to meet their sector's needs.

- The regional skills strategies produced by the RDAs which Regional Skills Partnerships – and their sub-regional partnerships – are using to ensure that the strategy for supply of skills, training, business support and labour market services is planned, managed and delivered in a coherent, collaborative way.

- the LSC's Business Cycle which provides the framework to integrate into a single streamlined process current and future regional skills needs into local and regional plans and funding arrangements.

215. But we feel that more needs to be done to translate these targets, priorities and pieces of architecture into a well understood and accepted resource allocation and distribution system.

WE RECOMMEND

- The building blocks, of a national learning model, and underpinning context and assumptions should be brought together into a single document which is published on a regular basis.

- This document should set out greater clarity about what the public purse will support in full, what the public purse will subsidise and what the Government considers individuals and employers might pay for in full.

- The Government should lead a national debate on this important issue which leads to a broader understanding with key stakeholders of the key principles underpinning public funding of learning, but also raises awareness about skills development and training amongst the wider general public.

- In certain circumstances government will need to stimulate the market and therefore proposals should be drawn up to consider how students/ trainees can be encouraged into shortage subjects.

A national debate on public funding for learning

216. The Government should lead promotional campaigns to help employers and learners understand the need for skills development and what their return on this investment will be. Colleges must play their part in ensuring that they prioritise the use of public funds on areas where the market cannot afford full cost funding. But this must be supported by national debate led by the Government and the LSC. This promotional activity and associated debate should also include further encouragement to employers to invest in skills development and this should be reinforced across Government. It will be vital that employers understand the direct benefits to their business productivity of skills development. But there is also a broader corporate responsibility issue for employers. We were surprised, for example, that the Government's vision for Corporate Social Responsibility (CSR), sponsored by the Department of Trade and Industry, does not include up-skilling the workforce as one of the CSR priorities. We recommend that skills should be a priority area under CSR. Our earlier recommendations for strengthening the integration at Government level should improve the skills focus across Government.

Funding systems and incentives – supporting the skills focus

217. The current funding system is complex, bureaucratic and causes difficulties for FE colleges and other providers.

218. Leaving aside the absolute volume of financial resource – whether there is enough to do the job – the way in which available resources are allocated and distributed clearly has a big impact on how relatively well local needs are met.

219. The LSC *agenda for change* proposals for a streamlined process, with a focus on plan, is to be welcomed – including the move away from the micro management of funding. These proposals, combined with the development of the NETP, and the capital and other funding incentives for greater specialisation and improving market entry, will help create a more responsive and demand led system.

220. The LSC should translate the national assessment, mentioned above, into allocations which focus resources and therefore learning activity into areas where it will make the greatest impact. As regional skills strategies are developed and informed by the Regional Skills Partnerships, the LSC would use these to determine local allocations to locality, reflecting local needs.

221. The expectation on the local setting would be to receive targets for participation, progress and skill accumulation in the local learning community and an appropriate quantum of resource. The regional level would be 'tight' on the delivery of achievement and local impact, but 'loose' on how the local LSC, and its local council, with local providers, configured activities to achieve such an impact. The emphasis would be on impact, not process.

Part 5
IMPROVING INSPECTION AND INFORMATION, REDUCING THE QUALIFICATIONS BUREAUCRACY

SECTION 5.1:
RATIONALISING THE INSPECTION REGIME

222. Good inspection systems are crucial to all modern public services. They keep the public informed, drive improvement, provide essential accountability to the public purse and enable comparisons of performance across services. But they must be clear, simple and operate within a framework of professional and modern management designed to maximise benefits and minimise waste. Inspection arrangements in the FE college system have been modernised in recent years, but it is important that they also keep pace with best practice in other public services.

The burden of inspection

223. Colleges are currently subject to an excessively high level of scrutiny

and inspection. The strict and highly centralised regime stems from the increased independence granted to colleges in the early 1990s followed by a few high-profile financial scandals and Government's growing concern about variability in the quality of college provision.

224. They are inspected by Ofsted (provision for young people) and ALI (work based learning and adult provision) and, until recently, all college inspections have been carried out to a standardised format regardless of performance and track record. A new Common Inspection Framework (CIF) was introduced by Ofsted and ALI this year along with more differentiated inspection arrangements, greater reliance on self assessment and more emphasis on supporting improvement in weaker colleges.

The case for simplification

225. Many colleges are also subject to various other inspection regimes including that of QAA for the HE work and Ofsted inspections of partner schools. They were included in the programme of area wide inspections of 14-19 provision and will be included in new joint area reviews, introduced by the Children's Act, next year. In addition, the LSC has its own annual provider reviews running to a separate timetable. Whilst Ofsted and ALI have made considerable efforts to coordinate their on-site visits to colleges, the overall burden is unnecessarily high. The proposal to create a single post-compulsory education Inspectorate would bring coherence, economies of scale and reduce some of the inherent bureaucracy felt by colleges, but better co-ordination with other regimes is also needed.

BOX 17

Ealing, Hammersmith and West London College

The use of technology is a strong feature of Ealing, Hammersmith and West London College's (EHWLC) culture. Information and data is 100% web based enabling lecturers, support staff and management to access information from anywhere at anytime. Data is collected from information input by staff and students themselves.

The system allows managers to model their curriculum for funding, aids course and room planning and enables lecturers to take control by enrolling and managing their students online. Lecturers mark registers online within the classroom which enables early intervention from student support officers, helping to improve student attendance and retention. This initiative has resulted in significant improvement in retention and progression in key areas, and has been highlighted by Ofsted as an example of good practice.

Students are allocated smart identity cards to access and leave the main campus, the learning centre and sports facilities. This provides information on levels and patterns of use of college facilities, to help with estates and facilities management planning. All full time students are supported by a tutorial system and three times a year tutors review students' progress on an on-line Individual Learning Plan.

Benefits include a significant improvement in the college's quality assurance processes. Electronic admission, enrolment, course approval and e-registers have removed the fraught, error-ridden intensive paper based systems. Senior managers conduct on-line self assessment reviews (SAR) with curriculum divisions, using the inspection format and all key performance reports are attached to their SAR. The emphasis has now shifted to quality issues in learning and teaching being at the heart and away from reams of paper and distrust in data.

More information can be found at EHWLC's website: www.centime3.co.uk

clear timelines introduced. This should include clear plans developed by the LSC for ensuring that all colleges have access to – possibly through shared services – state of the art management information systems along the lines of the EHWLC model. And so that colleges can see and look forward to a definite reduction in the data burden.

Single minded focus on information

237. We think there is a strong case for consideration to be given to a single purpose agency set up that collects and synthesises data. This role could be played by the Higher Education Statistics Agency (HESA), building on the role it plays for HE

or by the LSC building on its delivery role for Managing Information Across Partners (MIAP). By whatever means, there would be clear sense in a single agency covering both FE and HE. We have heard from many colleges, and particularly the mixed economy colleges, of the difficulty and bureaucracy involved in dealing with separate organisations for their provision. The rationale behind a single body is to give dedicated, focused urgency. The current position of poor information collection and use cannot be allowed to continue.

WE RECOMMEND

- The LSC, supported by the DfES, establishes clear information standards across the learning and skills sector including comparative data on value for money.

- In line with these standards, there must be urgent rationalisation and simplification of the data collected as a priority as it is at the heart of good management and resource utilisation.

- The Government should consider whether this role is best fulfilled by:
  - giving it to HESA;
  - giving it to the LSC; or
  - a single data agency covering both HE and FE and perhaps extending to other education sectors.

A key consideration would be the ability to deliver a more efficient system within 18 months.

- The LSC should develop plans to ensure that all colleges have access to – possibly through shared services – state of the art management information systems along the lines of the EHWLC model. Colleges should look forward to a definite reduction in the data burden.

SECTION 5.3: STREAMLINING THE QUALIFICATIONS PROCESS

238. A clear and simple qualifications system is essential if FE colleges are to help learners to make the best choices for progression to employment or higher education. The current qualifications system is confusing and complex with 115 Awarding Bodies and in excess of 5,000 qualifications in the National Qualifications Framework. The qualifications system is not easy for learners, employers and others to understand or navigate.

239. Despite the system for ascribing levels to qualifications, qualification equivalences are not clear either in relation to size or what a qualification enables you to do. We have also heard that the qualifications system is not sufficiently responsive to the needs of individuals, employers and communities. Colleges have told us that it is inflexible, dealing primarily in whole qualifications taken in full at one time. This does not allow, for example, the use of one or more units of a qualification to add to an employee's existing skills or update them, either because the qualification is not unit-based or because public funding and targets are tied to the national (full) qualifications.

240. We also heard concerns about how the qualifications system impeded progression to higher levels. Unlike Scotland and Wales, there is not yet a national credit system in England that aligns FE and HE qualifications to support a wider range of achievements to be recognised when progression is sought.

241. For colleges, the system is also time consuming and expensive and the bureaucracy involved great. Despite moves to decrease the assessment burden in the qualifications system, the assessment systems are still too demanding on teacher and learner time. Typically, colleges have to deal with many awarding bodies, sometimes up to 30. And the awarding body systems are not common.

A simplified framework

242. The broad approach of the proposed Framework for Achievement is a very welcome and rational development. When fully implemented, it should transform the qualifications scene with a flexible, unit-based framework, underpinned by credit, allowing qualifications to be built from nationally available units. This will help colleges in delivering rapid and relevant qualifications for the local labour market and FE colleges need to be able to influence the content of the new framework alongside employers and SSCs and through the sector qualification strategies. Colleges also need to be able to package units together to meet particular employer needs. But the pace of change towards the Framework for Achievement is too slow and we urge that it is accelerated.

243. We also think that over the medium term, as part of a move to self regulation, consideration should be given to allowing some colleges, that meet quality criteria the ability to award their own qualifications, rather than working through awarding bodies.

244. We also recommend that FE colleges, working as networks, use their purchasing power and develop consortia to negotiate costs with awarding bodies so that economies of scale can be realised. In addition we think there is scope for colleges to collaborate and negotiate with awarding bodies the rationalisation of a range of awarding bodies' administrative requirements. The QCA and awarding bodies also need to ensure that the Framework for Achievement does not result in more costs for FE colleges, either through increased charges for unit registration or through awarding bodies passing on the costs of developing infrastructures.

WE RECOMMEND

We recommend that:

- the QCA accelerates the pace of change towards the Framework for Achievement as it brings much needed clarification;

- the AoC should help identify the costs to colleges of dealing with awarding bodies;

- FE colleges should use their purchasing power and develop voluntary consortia to negotiate costs with awarding bodies so that economies of scale can be realised; and at the same time, seek rationalisation of awarding bodies' administrative requirements.

G
Ground

Part 6
IMPROVING INFRASTUCTURE

SECTION 6.1:
DEVELOPING THE WORKFORCE

245. Almost a quarter of a million people are currently employed in FE colleges across England. They are the most vital resource that FE colleges have. In the course of the review it was clear that focused, committed and professional lecturers, support staff and leaders have transformed individual lives and make a real difference to local businesses.

'I gave all my teachers a card, with a little essay in there of how they helped me because they all had their individual influence that's helped me to get where I've got'

Young male studying full time

246. Until recently there has been little coordinated national effort around workforce development. The Success for All reforms, including the qualification targets, are beginning to make a difference, but more needs to be done.

Challenges

247. The workforce, managers and leaders face many challenges. Many people who contributed to the Review were concerned about the workforce's age profile – almost a third of the workforce is over 50 – particularly in relation to its impact on the ability of FE colleges to attract new younger recruits and portray a dynamic image. Furthermore, improving the diversity of the workforce is a priority: for example only 6% of the workforce is known to be from black or minority ethnic groups compared to 14% of learners. And there

are even fewer people from black or minority ethnic groups amongst college leaders and managers, with less than 2% of principals coming from black or minority ethnic backgrounds. As mentioned in Section 3.1, none of the organisations supporting workforce and leadership development have black or minority ethnic staff in senior management positions. Since the Commission for Black Staff in FE reported in November 2002, a range of initiatives and activities have been implemented including the development of a new Race Equality Standards for FE and the Black Leadership Initiative. More needs to be done.

248. Worries were also frequently expressed about the casualisation of the workforce. A significant proportion of staff (over 17%) do not have permanent full time or part time contracts. There may be legitimate reasons for employing staff on this basis, particularly where FE colleges are supplementing their expertise with professionals working in industry and contributing specialist knowledge. But it does create a fragmented workforce and makes staff development and organisational transformation more difficult to manage.

249. Morale is strongly affected by a lack of parity of esteem and reward with other parts of the education system, particularly schools and HE. Support staff – many in quasi-teaching roles – feel particularly undervalued. And we received many representations about the impact of salary levels on colleges' ability to recruit and retain. Despite these major issues there is a passionate, committed and professional workforce in FE colleges across the country, who consistently score high levels of learner satisfaction.

250. In the future, particularly with the 14-19 and skills strategies changing the market for colleges, the need for high level management and leadership skills will extend. What is needed is a more systematic capacity and capability building push across the network around professional development.

A workforce strategy

251. There is already work in train to improve the quality and professional standing of the workforce and its leadership. This includes the implementation of teaching and learning reforms by the Standards Unit, work to improve initial teacher training, the work of the Centre of Excellence in Leadership, the establishment

of Lifelong Learning UK as the SSC responsible for developing standards for the sector, and the embryonic work of the Institute for Learning.

252. However, it is recommended that a new national workforce development strategy be produced, led by DfES, founded on a fresh analysis of workforce needs. This should have clear priorities and action plans and be available publicly in twelve months. We have outlined earlier in the quality section the changes we believe are necessary to improve the skills focus and relevance of teaching and support staff. This strategy should also include specific measures to address recruitment and retention in important skills gaps and review remuneration in key areas.

WE RECOMMEND

- The DfES, working with the AoC and FE colleges, should provide a clear and targeted workforce development strategy within the next twelve months which is published and consulted on prior to implementation.

- This strategy should record all of the key data concerning workforce numbers, ages, shortages, strengths and weaknesses.

- The strategy should spell out an approach to deal with:
  - improved and consistent continued professional development including improving vocational expertise;
  - practical solutions to deal with skill shortages;
  - a clear strategy for addressing the ageing workforce;

– market based solution to the concerns about current levels of pay.

College leadership

253. The national workforce development strategy proposed above should also include a clear plan for improving leadership and management across the sector. As we said earlier, strong and effective management and leadership makes a critical difference to quality and impact.

254. We met and heard of many able and impressive college principals and senior managers. But we also know from inspection evidence that management and leadership are insufficiently strong, taken in the round. There is not a good enough supply of leaders capable of getting the best from their staff and managing highly complex businesses. To lead the organisational transformation we propose in this report, FE colleges need very able, experienced and influential managers, firmly focused on priorities, quality, reputation, learners and outcomes.

255. Getting good managers in place is not a quick fix. It takes time, energy and resources. The Centre of Excellence in Leadership and other initiatives including the Black Leadership Initiative, have begun this process. The cost and accessibility of training and development remain issues. And FE colleges as a whole fail to attract new talent from outside (95% of principals come from a FE college background). The national workforce development strategy must set out clear plans for succession planning. It is important that the necessary

incentives, resources and impact measures are provided over the next two years to bring about a quantum leap in leadership development and performance (this will require a more interventionist approach to ensure that all colleges engage and support leadership development).

WE RECOMMEND

- The Government introduces clearer 'standards' and 'measures' for effective leadership that incentivise and reward outstanding work.

- The Government introduces new, radical approaches to bring in effective leaders from outside and ensure their success and impact. In the first instance it would be prudent to devise a programme to recruit and train 50 new senior middle managers a year from other sectors.

- The Government should consider how the synergies between National College for School Leadership, HE Leadership Foundation and CEL could be developed to simplify the leadership landscape, make best use of resources. And the Government should consider whether amalgamation is the best way of doing this.

- Government and colleges find a solution to make leadership development more affordable so more colleges engage.

WE RECOMMEND

- Capital investment plans follow, and do not determine, clearly defined FE college purposes.

- The opportunity is taken to use capital expenditure for local collaboration.

- Capital investment is much more closely aligned to national and regional strategies to meet vocational priorities, informed but not driven by a bottom-up analysis.

- DfES and LSC ensure that the use of e-learning and ICT in teaching and learning and across FE college business systems is actively promoted in their strategies.

- LSC and DfES to investigate how connectivity for colleges might continue to be supported.

- LSC and DfES, working with Becta and others, explore how to stimulate the market for content and increase the amount of good quality material available to FE colleges and give guidance on developing integrated systems and electronic campuses.

- Capital investment delivers sustainable development objectives.

Part 7
IMPLEMENTATION

SECTION 7.1:
MANAGING THE CHANGE

Implementation Unit

267. If the Government, FE colleges and the other key stakeholders agree that our recommendations are the right way forward, the manner of their implementation will be critical to success.

268. To ensure the coherent implementation of our recommendations, were they to be accepted, would require the setting up of a dedicated, time-limited Implementation Unit established jointly by the DfES and LSC.

269. Clearly we are not at the point of creating Terms of Reference but we can indicate what we believe would be the minimal success criteria for such a unit and its work.

270. It will be important to:

- establish a Steering Group comprising wide representation from the stakeholders.

- establish a user group including representatives of learners, employers and communities (e.g. local authorities).

- commit resources to the unit in recognition of the scale, complexity and importance of its change management task.

- appoint a clearly accountable single signing officer (who chairs the Steering Group) accountable for the outcomes of the project against its terms of reference, reporting to a Minister of State.

- set up a project team that should include a mix of internal (from DfES and LSC) and external skills (including FE colleges) and the following roles at a minimum:

  - Project Director (internal), accountable to the Steering Group for the delivery of the project against its strategic objectives; and

  - Policy Analysts / 'thinkers', organisation design expert(s).

271. Key features of the new unit will include:

- a clear 'stakeholder management' and communication strategy to be developed and actioned from the beginning so that colleges feel involved and informed.

- ensuring coherence and integration with existing reforms planned, including the LSC's *agenda for change*.

- excellent project management discipline (milestones, deliverables, etc).

- skilful brokerage with key players.

272. An important part of the unit's work will be to keep FE colleges informed and to encourage them to be proactive and take early action over what needs to be done.

273. The successful operation of this joint unit will be a critical test of the new, open and trust based relationship between LSC and DfES.

Part 8
SUMMARY OF RECOMMENDATIONS

SECTION 8.1:
RECOMMENDATIONS

This section sets out the recommendations by stakeholder. Where possible we have attempted to assign leads, but some recommendations appear more than once as a number of stakeholders need to take them forward. **The recommendations which are imperatives are shown in bold for ease of reference.** The other recommendations are important, supporting recommendations.

Colleges and college corporations

Vision *(pages 1-4)*

- FE colleges and their corporations should review how they compare against the description of the FE college of the future and act on the outcome.

- FE college principals – and aspiring managers and leaders – should review how well they meet the competencies described for leaders of the future and consider the further experience and development they need.

Purpose imperative *(pages 13-22)*

- **GFEC and tertiary colleges should adopt as their primary purpose, improving employability and supplying economically valuable skills.**

- **To achieve this: the skills focus should be clear in mission statements, there must be a rigorous approach to quality, and funding incentives, performance management arrangements, capital investment and workforce development strategies must all be geared towards this primary purpose.**

- There should be a stronger push, supported by incentives, to develop vocational specialisms within General FE and tertiary colleges. These should be connected through hub and spoke arrangements across the country embracing the new Skills Academies and a revised CoVE programme.

- Sixth form colleges should retain their primary focus of academic achievement and progression for 16-19 year olds, and be treated by the DfES and LSC as a distinctive brand.

- FE colleges, working collaboratively with Higher Education Institutions, should improve learner pathways to higher education to facilitate progression.

Quality imperative *(pages 22-29)*

- **There must be a continued drive by colleges to improve quality and achieve excellence. Failing provision must be addressed and coasting provision should strive for excellence.**

- **Self Regulation should be the medium term goal. Colleges should work with the LSC and QIA, to develop the foundations for this based on a new model of self assessment underpinned by broader measures of impact and value for money. Those colleges that demonstrate the achievement of criteria for such as system, should over time increasingly be rewarded with greater autonomy.**

- **FE colleges should strive for long term, continuous improvements in teaching and learning based on best practice from across the sector.**

- **FE colleges must address more urgently provision which is failing, supported by the LSC, QIA and others.**

Learner imperative *(pages 29-34)*

274. All colleges should improve the way they engage and listen to learners and act on the outcomes. Specific recommendations:

- **FE colleges should be required to collect learners' views in a consistent and systematic manner as a key way of improving college provision.**

- FE colleges should consult learners on major issues impacting on their learning and the learner

environment. This should be part of the learner entitlement.

- FE Colleges should be required to publish annually this information in a learner report, together with their plans for addressing the issues.

275. This will be a key part of any move towards greater self regulation.

The employer imperative *(pages 34-38)*

276. Colleges need to improve their services to employers. The key recommendations in the report about a skills focus should help achieve this. In addition:

- **FE colleges should look at what more they need to do to improve their offer to employers both through their primary role in improving the pool of employability and skills and in response to specific employer needs.**

- FE colleges should work with the LSC to develop a network of 'business' colleges focused on the needs of employers as proposed under *agenda for change*. This should include developing the new national standard in the design and delivery of workforce development service to employers.

The reputation imperative *(pages 38-40)*

- **All FE colleges should be active locally in promoting their services and the college brand and vision to local stakeholders.**

- Some principals, for example of larger colleges, should take on a promotional role at regional and national level.

277. At the heart will be the need to simplify and explain how society will benefit. It will also be important that staff working in FE colleges leave behind concerns of the past and move to project the extended benefit they will bring.

Local provision *(pages 41-45)*

- FE colleges should work together (and with other providers) to improve learning pathways and choice (including for the 14-19 phase) and to realise the opportunities for economies of scale, development and innovation.

- These networks should have as a core objective improving information, advice and guidance to help learners and employers navigate around local provision.

- Successful local colleges and other providers should be allowed to grow through an increasingly more contestable and open learning market.

A clear separation of functions *(pages 45-47)*

- FE colleges should have as their core function the provision of high quality, value for money services for learners and employers. They should play an active part in helping the local commissioner develop the overall local strategy, but there should be a clear and unambiguous separation from the local commissioning function.

- FE college governance arrangements should not be changed, but FE colleges and the Government should take steps to improve the diversity of governing bodies. There should also be a guide to good Governance to underpin the

new purpose and clarify roles and responsibilities.

Improving information *(pages 59-61)*

- **All colleges should have access to state of the art management information systems and be actively using this information – including inter-college comparative value for money data – to manage their organisations.**

Streamlining the qualifications process
(pages 61-62)

- The AoC should help identify the costs to colleges of dealing with awarding bodies.

- FE colleges should use their purchasing power and develop voluntary consortia to negotiate costs with awarding bodies so that economies of scale can be realised.

- FE Colleges should also use their collective purchasing power to negotiate with awarding bodies the rationalisation of their administrative requirements.

Developing the workforce and leadership
(pages 63-65)

- There should be a more systematic capacity and capability building push across the college network around professional development.

- FE Colleges should work with the DfES to develop a new national workforce development strategy founded on a fresh analysis of workforce needs. And implement its proposals.

- Government and colleges find a solution to make leadership development more affordable so more colleges engage.

- Colleges should work with the Government on a programme to introduce new, radical approaches to develop leadership and to bring in effective leaders in from outside the college system. In the first instance it would be prudent to devise a programme to recruit and train 50 new senior middle managers a year from other sectors.

Improving the estate and IT *(pages 66-68)*

- Colleges should ensure that their capital investment plans follow, and do not determine, their clearly defined purposes. They should also support the extension of e-learning, ICT and community outreach and also deliver sustainable development objectives.

The Learning and Skills Council

Vision *(pages 1-4)*

- **The LSC should consider what more it needs to do to transform its planning, funding and accountability systems so that they meet the aspirations set out in the vision.**

Purpose imperative *(pages 13-22)*

- LSC should support the skills imperative by ensuring funding and performance management systems are aligned with it, that there are proper incentives. They should support the further development of specialisms, including a reformed CoVE programme.

- The LSC should treat sixth form colleges as distinctive brand.

- The LSC should continue its work with HEFCE to improve learner pathways to higher education to facilitate progression.

Equality and diversity *(pages 20-23)*

- The Learning and Skills Council should give consideration to implementing the recommendations of its review of learners with learning difficulties and/or disabilities – carried out by Peter Little.

- The Learning and Skills Council should recruit the services of a senior executive search firm who will specialise in strengthening the numbers of employees from diverse backgrounds coming forward for competitive interviews in non executive and senior management roles across the sector.

- The Learning and Skills Council should support general programmes of diversity awareness training within the sector.

Quality imperative *(pages 22-29)*

- The LSC should develop, with the sector, an intensive development programme for one year for under-performing colleges who are in the failing category. Those colleges or departments that do not pass a re-inspection should be made the subject of a contestability review, organised by the LSC, which could result in the removal of services, changes in management or the closure of the college.

- The LSC and QIA should develop a new self-assessment model for colleges as a foundation for movement towards to self-regulation. It should be based upon a broader set of measures of success and indicators of impact, and a set of benchmarks including value for money. This should build on the proposals in *agenda for change*.

Learner imperative *(pages 29-34)*

- The LSC should ensure that its planning, funding and performance management arrangements take full account of the voice of learners.

- It should introduce a requirement for FE colleges to collect learners' views on their learning and the learner environment in a consistent and systematic way as a key way of improving college provision. Colleges should be required to publish annually this information in a learner report, together with their plans for addressing the issues. The LSC should aggregate this nationally and publish it.

- The LSC should establish learner panels to provide a stronger learner voice in determining local needs.

The Employer imperative *(pages 34-38)*

- The LSC should continue with its plans under *agenda for change* to create a national network of colleges and other providers which are focused on the needs of employers.

- The Government and the LSC should consider what further action should be taken to improve engagement between colleges and employers when it receives the advice of the Leitch Review of Skills next year.

The Reputation imperative *(pages 38-40)*

- The LSC should promote widely the new purpose, brand and benefits of FE colleges.

Local provision *(pages 41-45)*

- The LSC, as local commissioner, should ensure the development of managed provider networks at local level is co-ordinated across the country in a systematic, in particular

to support the Government's 14-19 plans.

- Capital support and help with initial start-up costs should be provided in special circumstances to prospective providers to assist market entry.

- It should introduce a requirement on colleges to collaborate (part of a wider Government requirement on all providers to collaborate) to make this happen. And it should provide financial incentives to local networks and to individual FE colleges to cover the initial cost of forming provider networks for sharing services. It should also introduce a requirement on FE colleges and other providers to provide an objective, shared service to help learners find appropriate courses.

- There must also be significant collaboration between the local authority and the local LSC, with absolute clarity at local level of roles and responsibilities.

- The LSC should continue with moves to open up the market and make it more contestable.

- The LSC should ensure all tenders and competitions are advertised regionally, and in some cases nationally, to allow national providers, other providers, or indeed colleges outside the local area to bid for new provision.

A clear separation of functions *(pages 45-47)*

- The LSC should ensure, as part of its *agenda for change* reforms, that local LSCs implement the commissioning functions set out in page 46,

- The LSC should develop its operational leadership role of the system, including a key regional role between the national body and localities.

Improving information *(pages 59-61)*

- The LSC, supported by the DfES, establishes and publishes clear information standards across the learning and skills sector including inter-college comparative data on value for money.

- In line with these standards, the LSC, with the DfES, should ensure urgent rationalisation and simplification of the data collected as a priority as it is at the heart of good management and resource utilisation.

- The LSC should develop plans to ensure that all colleges have access to – possibly through shared services – state of the art management information systems.

Improving the estate and IT *(pages 66-68)*

- The LSC should ensure that capital investment plans follow, and do not determine, clearly defined FE college purposes. This should include using capital expenditure for local collaboration and community outreach.

- It should ensure capital investment is much more closely aligned to national and regional strategies to meet vocational priorities, informed by, but not driven by, a bottom up analysis.

The Government and DfES

Purpose imperative *(pages 13-22)*

- **The Government should articulate a core role for FE colleges, in particular GFECs, in supplying economically valuable skills.**

- The Government should recognise that a primary focus on skills does not exclude other significant purposes in promoting social inclusion and facilitating progression.

- The skills focus should be supported by policies on payment for courses should be explored.

College governance *(pages 45-46)*

- College governance arrangements should not be changed. But the Government should take steps to improve the diversity of Governing bodies and they should also develop a guide to good Governance.

Equality and diversity *(pages 20-23)*

- The Government should appoint an independent organisation to review the recruitment processes for Chairs of FE colleges to assess their effectiveness and make recommendations to the Government.

The Quality imperative *(pages 22-29)*

- The Government and the QIA should ensure long term continuous improvements in teaching and learning by extending the national teaching and learning change programme to cover other key areas.

- **The Government should further rationalise the oversight, inspection and accreditation bodies.**

- **The Government should expedite plans to relocate the Standards Unit resources to the QIA**

- The Government should introduce compulsory return to business/ industry refresher up-skilling weeks for all vocational lecturers.

- The Government's CSR agenda should be expanded to cover employers encouraging their employees to take an active part in skills training either by being assessors and or becoming visiting lecturers/trainers in colleges.

- The Government should consider a new policy for giving incentives to those in employment to become vocational tutors and visiting lecturers.

- The Government should ensure that the new qualifications requirement on all college lecturers is not placing too many barriers in the way of vocational specialists entering teaching. The qualification framework should be reviewed and a new category of vocational tutor should be developed.

- The Government should consider undertaking value for money studies, including asset utilisation, and bringing forward proposals for efficiencies in procurement.

The learner imperative (pages 29-34)

- The Government should expedite its reforms of information, advice and guidance to improve services to learners.

- The Government and LSC should introduce a requirement on providers to provide an objective shared service to help learners find appropriate courses (part of their requirement to collaborate).

- The Government should ensure that there is more training for learner representatives in colleges to ensure they are equipped to participate effectively.

The employer imperative (pages 34-38)

- The Government and the LSC should sustain its programme of reforms including the Skills Strategy and the LSC's agenda for change, but these should be reviewed in the light of the Leitch recommendations.

- The Government should extend union initiatives to improve skills development including the new Academy and Union Learning Representatives.

- The Government should consider establishing local or regional Work and Skills Boards of senior employers to Regional Skills Partnerships identify gaps in the supply and demand for skills.

The reputation imperative (pages 38-40)

- The Government should promote widely the clear purpose and strong brand for FE linked to the skills mission and there needs to be a long term consistency in this promotion;

- **The Government should lead a review of reputation, working with the LSC and the AoC.**

Local provision (pages 41-45)

- With the LSC, the Government should ensure that the development of managed provider networks at local level are co-ordinated across the country in a systematic way, in particular, to support the Government's 14-19 plans. There should be a new requirement on all providers to collaborate to make this happen.

- As a matter of principle, Government should ensure that the different systems and information sources that exist to help people navigate learner pathways are made more learner focused, understandable and accessible to improve choice.

- With the LSC, the Government should introduce a requirement on providers to provide a shared service to help learners and appropriate courses (part of the requirement to collaborate).

The strategic architect *(pages 47-48)*

- **The Government should set the vision for FE and this should be in the context of a wide educational strategy covering all sector. This should be translated through the LSC and interpreted locally by colleges and other partners.**

- The Government should give a stronger focus and interest in colleges and what they can offer.

- The Government should review the way that the corporate leadership for skills is organised with the intention of enhancing the importance of the role.

- The Government should establish a yearly review of activity at regional level and hold the system to account. (To be conducted by an independent scrutiny body).

- The Permanent Secretary should consider leading bi-annual conferences with the director generals and the heads of agencies and other non-departmental bodies to focus on learner benefit and national interest, with an emphasis on joined-up policy and operations.

Funding *(pages 53-55)*

- **The Government should bring together building blocks, of a national learning model spanning schools, FE and HE,**

and underpinning context and assumptions into a single document which is published on a regular basis.

- This document should set out greater clarity about what the public purse will support in full, what the public purse will subsidise and what the Government considers individuals and employers might pay for in full.

- The Government should lead a national debate on this important issue which leads to a broader understanding with key stakeholders of the key principles underpinning public funding of learning, but also raises awareness about skills development and training amongst the wider general public.

- in certain circumstances, the Government should stimulate the market and consider how learners can be encouraged in shortage subjects.

Improving information *(pages 59-61)*

- There must be urgent rationalisation and simplification of the data collected as a priority as it is at the heart of good management and resource utilisation.

- **The Government should consider whether this role is best fulfilled by:**

  - **giving it to HESA;**

  - **giving it to the LSC; or**

  - **a single data agency covering both HE and FE and perhaps extending to other education sectors.**

278. A key consideration would be the ability to deliver a more efficient system within 18 months.

Developing the workforce *(pages 63-65)*

- **The Government, with the AoC and FE colleges and other key stakeholders, should develop a clear and targeted workforce development plan within the next twelve months which is published and consulted on prior to implementation.**

- This plan should record all of the key data concerning the workforce numbers, ages, shortages, strengths and weaknesses.

- The plan should spell out an approach:

  - improved and consistent continued professional development including improving vocational expertise.

  - practical solutions to deal with skill shortages.

  - a clear strategy for addressing the ageing workforce.

  - a market based solution to the concerns about current levels of pay.

- The Government should introduce clearer "standards" and "measures" of leadership.

- The Government should introduce new, radical approaches to bring effective leaders in from outside the college system and ensure their success and impact. In the first instance it would be prudent to devise a programme to recruit and train 50 new senior middle managers a year from other sectors.

- The Government should consider how the synergies between National College for School Leadership, HE Leadership Foundation and CEL could be developed to simplify the leadership landscape, and make best use of resources. And the Government should consider whether amalgamation is the best way of doing this.

- The Government, with FE colleges should find a solution to make the leadership development more affordable so more colleges engage.

The LSC and the DfES

Clarity in roles and relationships *(pages 51-53)*

- The central roles of the LSC and DfES should be refined so as to lighten the impact of centralised control and monitoring and minimise duplication and undue central demands.

- The roles of the LSC and DfES need to be clear and complementary and this should be translated into a relationship based on trust and openness.

- LSC and the DfES should review their formal concordat to ensure the clarity proposed above is in place.

- LSC and DfES and other organisations take further steps to ensure that more resources are relocated to services for learners.

Improving the estate and IT *(pages 66-68)*

- DfES and LSC ensure that the use of e-learning and ICT in teaching and learning and across colleges' business systems is actively promoted across the range of their strategies.

- LSC and DfES should investigate how internet connectivity for colleges might continue to be supported.

- LSC and DfES, working with Becta and others, should explore how to stimulate the market for content and increase the amount of good quality material available and give guidance on developing integrated systems and electronic campuses.

Implementation *(page 69)*

- **A dedicated, time-limited Implementation Unit should be established under an experienced General Manager as Project Director, with the task of putting significant changes in place within 18 months.**

- This Unit should be monitored by a national stakeholder group.

The LSC and HEFCE

- **HEFCE and LSC, colleges and universities should expedite work to ensure clear learner pathways exist across the country to enable progression to higher levels.**

The inspectorates and improvement bodies

- The CEL and other partners should expedite and augment the Black Leadership Initiative and the outstanding recommendations of the Commission for Black Staff in FE.

- **The new QIA should consult widely on the quality improvement strategy and then publish it as a firm framework for implementation by colleges**

- The QIA and CEL in Leadership should give major support to those institutions who are failing or coasting.

- There should be a single inspectorate and the ALI corporate knowledge and experience should be celebrated and embedded within the new organisation.

- the new inspection organisation should develop a "state of the art" inspection methodology which incorporates the learner experience, corporate governance, comparative performance, impact and value for money criteria, alongside the essential quality and outcome measures.

- This inspection activity should also include a strong element of area assessment, community and business impact.

Qualifications and Curriculum Authority (QCA)

- The QCA accelerates the pace of change towards the Framework of Achievement as it brings much needed clarification.

Employers

- Employers need to think more systematically about their medium term skill needs and discuss these with their local college or other provider.

APPENDIX 1: **THE FE LANDSCAPE**

WHAT IS THE FE COLLEGE SECTOR

The current statutory FE college sector comprises of a number of different 'types' of institutions, and within these broad organisational forms, there are wide differences in size and focus. The key categories, with descriptions, are set out below:

- **GFECs and tertiary colleges** offer a broad range of vocational and academic subjects at different levels and cater for both young people and adults. There are around 250 across England. Their strength is in offering a broad range of provision in one setting. GFECs are diverse with complex and varied patterns of provision – a result of shifting national priorities over the past 12 years and different local needs and institutional arrangements. At their best they offer individually tailored ladders of opportunity from entry level up to higher education, rooted in local community needs. Tertiary colleges are a distinctive model. There are around 50 in England. Although they are not recognised as a separate category in official statistics, we received many representations about their strengths. Recent research by the Responsive College Unit claims that their success rates are at least as good as sixth form colleges and that they significantly out perform GFECs at all levels except entry level.

- **Sixth form colleges** have traditionally catered for 16-19 year olds following A-level courses, but most have now broadened their curriculum and student profile. There are around 100 across England. They have a well evidenced track record in the delivery of full time provision for 16-19 year olds (their success rates are high at 76% in 2003/04). Yet the current planning system has created only two new sixth form colleges since incorporation.

- **Specialist colleges** concentrate on specialist curriculum areas e.g. art and design and land based subjects. Because of their focus on particular sectors, they have well established links with employers and industry in their sector. There are 22 across England.

- **Specialist designated institutions**, cater mainly for adults and a number are residential. There are 16 in England.

Over recent years the number of FE sector colleges has fallen considerably. There were around 460 FE colleges created at incorporation in 1993.

Colleges also vary considerably in size. The average number of learners at a GFEC is 12,000; the largest has over 45,000, the smallest has only 2,500. Sixth form colleges vary also: from around 570 to over 7,000 learners. The largest colleges have significant resources with annual budgets of up to £65 million. Specialist colleges

Composition of the FE college sector
The current statutory FE college sector comprises of a number of different 'types' of institutions

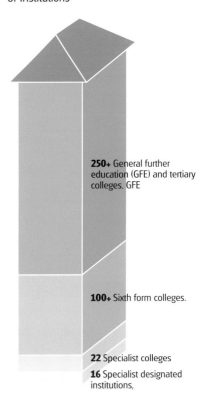

250+ General further education (GFE) and tertiary colleges. GFE

100+ Sixth form colleges.

22 Specialist colleges

16 Specialist designated institutions,

Source: DfES

tend to be smaller – for example the average funding allocation by the LSC for art and design colleges is £3.1 million. Most colleges get the majority of their income from public sources: on average 78% comes from the LSC, with 9% from fees from employers or individuals.

LEARNERS IN COLLEGES

Over 3 million learners attend GFEC and tertiary colleges every year and 229,000 attend sixth form colleges. The majority of enrolments are adults (aged over 19) studying on a part time basis (though the position in sixth form colleges is very different with the majority of enrolments (56%) under 19 studying on a full time basis). If we look at teaching hours however, the picture looks very different. Roughly half of GFEC and tertiary college provision is for 16-18

year olds and half is for adults. Long vocational courses (courses over 24 weeks) are the main form of learning at these colleges.

[TABLE 1] shows LSC funded learners in the FE sector (colleges and external institutions) by age, mode of attendance and gender since 1996/97.

Learner numbers in 2003/04 were 668,000, (19%) higher than in 1996/97. The expansion in numbers is predominantly in adult learners and the over 60 age group has seen a particularly significant increase (more than trebled since 1996/97). The number of full time learners in 2003/04 is virtually unchanged from 1996/97 – part time learners account for the increase in numbers over the period.

The increase in the number of female learners (+27%) outstrips the increase in the number of male learners (+10%).

TABLE 1

Learners (000) by age, mode of attendance and gender (LSC funded)

	1996/97	1997/98	1998/99	1999/00	2000/01	2001/02	2002/03	2003/04
By age:								
Below 19	676	672	646	634	625	647	687	701
19-59	2,585	2,600	2,501	2,409	2,503	2,873	3,084	3,001
60 and over	113	122	129	166	234	314	399	387
Age unknown	72	52	40	37	40	34	28	25
By mode of attendance:								
Full-time full-year	717	690	670	667	638	636	691	700
Other full-time	233	247	233	205	213	246	237	231
Part-time	2,497	2,510	2,413	2,374	2,552	2,986	3,270	3,184
By gender:								
Female	1,952	1,935	1,899	1,886	2,006	2,288	2,506	2,475
Male	1,495	1,512	1,416	1,359	1,396	1,580	1,691	1,639
Total	3,446	3,447	3,315	3,246	3,402	3,868	4,197	4,114

This has further shifted the gender mix in favour of females (1996/97 females = 57% learners; 2003/04 females = 60% learners).

In 2003/04, 78% of learners in FE colleges were from white ethnic groups, 14% were from non-white ethnic groups and 7.5% were 'not known/not provided'. Adults from non-white ethnic groups account for 8% of the adult population.

Colleges have more learners (both 16-19 and adult) who are relatively disadvantaged compared to the population as a whole and to learner populations in other educational establishment types. The proportion of GFEC learners who reside in Widening Participation (WP) postcodes[1] is 29%, compared to 25% of the population. The proportion in sixth form colleges is 25%. The figures for school sixth forms and higher education are 19% and 20% respectively. And according to the Youth Cohort Survey (2002), for 16 and 17 year olds in full time education, 45% of 16 year olds in full time learning have parents in the bottom 3 National Statistics socio-economic classes (NS-SEC). In GFECs 56% come from those groups, and 42% in sixth form colleges (the figure for state schools is 41%).

SUCCESS RATES

Assessments of quality in colleges are currently based on three measures: inspection evidence, learner success rates and learner satisfaction levels. The headline current position is:

- Inspection evidence. About 90% of provision is regarded as satisfactory or better. But there is not yet a clear improving trend in quality.

- Learner success rates. These have improved quite significantly – from 59% in 2000/01 to 72% in 2003/04 [FIGURE 6]. However, these averages conceal huge variations between individual colleges and between individual subject areas.

- Learner satisfaction evidence. Learners report that they are satisfied with the learning they receive in colleges. 90% of learners say they are satisfied with their current learning experience.

Across the range of provision performance at level 3, especially A levels, has the highest success rates, but even here the results vary by subject (67% for ICT and 81% for English). Performance at level 2 is still very poor – only 52% of 16-18 year olds starting level 2 courses gained a full qualification in 2002/03. And inspection evidence also shows that courses at entry level and levels 1 and 2 continue to be less well taught than courses at level 3 and above. Retention rates have remained pretty stable (83% in 2001/02 and 85% in 2003/04) though rates for vocational courses for young people are still low – 68% in 2002/03.

There is a perception that the headline success rate has increased because of a narrowing of the success rate gap between the 'worst' and 'best' colleges. This does not appear to be true – success rate improvement has been at the bottom and top end of the distribution. For GFEC and sixth form colleges the success rate gap between

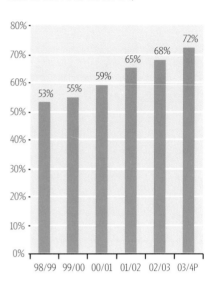

FIGURE 6

FE colleges headline learner success rate 1997/98 to 2003/04)

Source: DfES

---

[1]   A WP uplift is payable for a variety of reasons, but the most common is when a learner lives in a postcode which is relatively disadvantaged. In 2002/03, 34% of FE learners received WP uplift, and 29% lived in WP postcodes.

the top and bottom performing colleges (defined as the 90th percentile and 10th percentile respectively) has narrowed only very slightly over the period 1998/99-2002/03.

There is a gap in performance between average headline success rates for GFECs and those for sixth form colleges (67% and 76% respectively). However, when we looked at this gap it can largely be explained by provision type and prior qualifications of learners. Other characteristics of learners in GFECs, such as motivation and social environment (sense of failure at 16, culture that is less positive to education) may explain much of the difference.

APPENDIX 2: **A VIEW FROM ABROAD**

UNITED STATES

Outline of the US Community College system

Community colleges are a uniquely American institution. They have a history of providing educational opportunities to all Americans. There are 1,132 community colleges in the United States and each is unique. But the overwhelming majority share the common mission of open access and equity, comprehensive programme offerings, community control and a commitment to teaching and lifelong learning. Community colleges have a remarkably diverse student profile [FIGURE 7]:

- 46% of all African-American students in higher education study in community colleges;

- 55%of all Hispanic students in higher education study in community colleges;

- 46% of all Asian/Pacific islanders in higher education study in community colleges;

- 58% of all female students in higher education study in community colleges, as do 46% of all college freshmen.

The average age of a community college student is 29 and they pay an average tuition fee of $1,518 per semester. Most community colleges have transfer agreements with universities by which the university accepts the associate degree as 2 years of credit towards a four year degree. 64% of university students now enter via this community college route.

Strengths and Key Differences from the English System

A key feature of the community college system is the **strong emphasis on self regulation and the lack of top down control.** There is no formal inspection process, national funding regime or national qualifications system. There are many university features in the community college system including their ownership of the Associate Degree. All credit bearing programmes count towards the Associate Degree which also allows earlier certificated stepping off points for certain professional qualifications.

Quality assurance arrangements often rely on peer assessment and the importance of retaining the confidence and respect of universities.

These close links with universities provide **clear pathways and progression routes for learners**.

The link with the high status State Universities which sometimes include common governance arrangements helps community colleges and their leaders enjoy **a positive reputation and high level of esteem**. They have in the AACC a powerful national association that manages the reputation of the community colleges and promotes it to state and national media and to government. College leaders are often powerful mediators

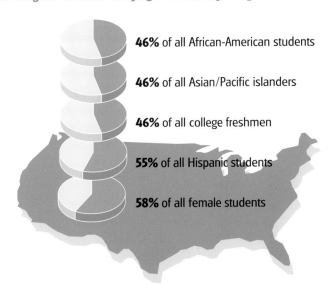

FIGURE 7

Students in higher education studying in community colleges in North America

46% of all African-American students

46% of all Asian/Pacific islanders

46% of all college freshmen

55% of all Hispanic students

58% of all female students

Source: DfES

with state governments, especially on funding.

The community is the driver for community colleges whose key focus is on skills and economic development for the community.

Issues of Transferability for the FE College System

Community colleges appear to achieve a high level of quality and standing without the heavy central control and complex accountability arrangements operating in our FE college system. Removing some of the multiple controls, introducing greater autonomy, self-regulation and peer assessment and developing more trust within the system are features worth considering further.

The possibility of enabling colleges to award Foundation Degrees and the development of an overarching credit framework could provide more coherence to vocational progression routes within FE through levels 3, 4 and 5.

A strong and effective representative organisation for FE colleges could be a powerful force in raising the profile and reputation of colleges with the media, government and stakeholders.

DENMARK

Outline of the Upper Secondary System

The Danish education system consists of three levels: basic schools, youth education and higher education. Youth education is the term used for upper secondary education and can be divided into three routes:

- Academically oriented upper secondary or 'gymnasium' route, broadly similar to our sixth form colleges.

- Vocationally oriented upper secondary or Vocational Education and Training (VET) route. There are approximately 128 colleges which are divided into four groups: technical colleges (32), business colleges (58), agricultural colleges (15) and social and health care colleges (23).

- Special individual education and training route, including production schools offering vocational preparation and work experience for people under the age of 25.

Approximately 50% of young people follow the academic route and 40-45% follow the vocational routes. Between 5-10% do not complete a qualifying youth education programme [FIGURE 8].

FIGURE 8

Course followed by upper secondary education students in Denmark

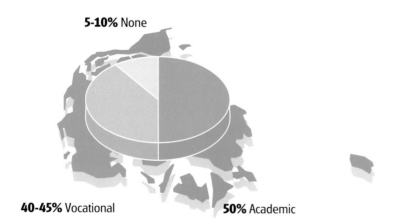

5-10% None

40-45% Vocational

50% Academic

Source: DfES

Strengths and Key Differences from the English System

Learner feedback is used extensively in the quality assurance process. As part of the legal requirement for a self evaluation methodology, colleges are required to conduct annual learner satisfaction surveys and post the results alongside retention and achievement data on their website. Self evaluation data is scrutinised by the Ministry who will investigate and take punitive action, where appropriate, if performance is judged to be poor.

Employer involvement is integral to vocational qualification design. Trade committees (equivalent to SSCs in the UK) define competence requirements for each occupational area. They also provide industry update training for tutors.

All colleges have a **common administration/management information system** and all learners (and citizens) have a unique identification number which has the capacity to follow educational participation, achievement and progression. This enables **learners to move flexibly around the system and supports the personalised learning approach**.

There is a much simpler management and accountability system than in England with no planning and funding body, independent inspectorate or awarding bodies. Funding is channelled from the Ministry to institutions and indirectly through the municipalities.

Issues of Transferability for the FE College System

The Danish personalised learning approach provides a good example of how the concept of personalisation might be applied to teaching and learning to help improve learners' experiences of post compulsory learning and skills in the UK.

The central management information system and unique identification number tracks learner attendance, participation, achievement and progression. Lessons can be learnt from the Danish system that largely reflects development work currently underway in the UK to create a learner registration service and unique learner number.

Though the Danish VET system has nationally recognised competencies and qualifications, there is scope within the system to allow colleges to tailor programmes of learning to reflect local demand.

The involvement of stakeholders is an important feature of the Danish approach to quality assurance and development. The requirement to conduct learner surveys, publish results and use them in evaluating performance and planning provision could, relatively easily, be incorporated into the English system. The systematic involvement of social partners (similar to trade unions) and employers in designing courses, working with colleges and providing information on labour market changes is worth further examination.

The Danish approach to quality assurance and development suggests that lighter touch inspection alongside a greater level of self assessment and customer feedback is worth serious consideration in the context of current proposals to move to greater self regulation in the English FE college system.

AUSTRALIA

Outline of the Vocational Education System

The Vocational Education and Training (VET) system in Australia enrols over 1.5 million students annually. This includes over 500,000 enrolments in New South Wales (NSW). The majority of enrolments in NSW are with the Institutes of Technical and Further Education (TAFE). VET students follow vocational programs such as engineering, business studies and adult basic education. Some students undertake the secondary school leaving certificate, the Higher School Certificate or its TAFE accredited alternative. Apprenticeship enrolments have increased by 28% since 2002 and there are now more than 45,000 apprentices currently undertaking off the job training with TAFE in NSW.

The gender split of TAFE NSW enrolments is around 50/50. Thirty three per cent of student enrolments are learners with learning difficulties and disabilities and/or learners from non-English speaking backgrounds. Twenty six per cent of TAFE students are under 19, although the majority are aged 24, with a growth in those aged 30-40.

Over 90% of TAFE students study part-time. and success rates are approximately 80%. In 2004 the module completion rate was 79.5% compared to 71.4% in 2000. Course

completions in NSW are approximately 50%.

Strengths and Key Differences from the English System

All **vocational qualifications are competency based** and contained in industry specific training packages. Industry Training Advisory Bodies (similar to Sector Skill Councils in the UK) develop specified competencies which are mapped against levels of qualification (four levels of Certificate and two levels of Diploma). The characteristics of these qualifications are also mapped against school and higher education qualifications in the Australian Qualifications Framework (AQF).

There is a much simpler accreditation and accountability system in Australia. With no awarding bodies or national inspectorates in Australia, there is a National Training Quality Framework Committee (NTQC) which oversees accreditation authorities who give providers Registered Training Organisation status to award vocational qualifications.

Since the 1990s, 100 colleges have been merged into 10 Institutes of Technical and Further Education which have on average over 50,000 enrolments, over 1,000 teaching staff and budgets over £65 million per annum. The Institute model has been copied throughout Australia. Enrolling in total over half a million students a year in NSW and over 1 million nationally, these Institutes deliver over 80% of publicly funded accredited training.

It has been government policy to develop a competitive training market at national and state levels as a means of increasing the efficiency and effectiveness of the VET system.

A user choice system has been introduced for structured apprenticeship and traineeship programs. Under the user choice system, funding flows to the training provider chosen by the employer and theoretically the employee.

Issues of Transferability for the FE College System

The modular, flexible structure of competency based training packages, combined with a tradition of flexible delivery and e-learning encourages greater flexibility and enables students to be enrolled throughout the educational year.

The Australian VET system is focused on work related education and training. It targets learners of all ages and there is no priority for 16-19 year olds.

Without awarding bodies and independent inspectorates, the Australian education system appears less bureaucratic with more resources targeted at delivery.

Quality assurance is largely about compliance and checking whether systems and procedures meet defined standards and there is relatively little focus on the inspection of delivery and the detailed achievement of learners.

Though university and TAFE qualifications are under the aegis of the AQF, some universities are reluctant to accept competency based TAFE qualifications. NSW however, has graded assessment in a competency based framework that goes some

way to meeting objections from the universities.

NETHERLANDS

Outline of the Secondary Vocational and Adult Education System

Secondary vocational and adult education in the Netherlands caters for around 600,000 students a year and is organised through 42 Regional Training Centres (ROCs). ROCs are essentially local monopoly providers with the learning delivered through specialist faculties or institutes. There are also a few specialist agricultural training centres but the number is reducing as they are absorbed by ROCs. There are two modes of secondary vocational education: a school based system (80% classroom) and apprenticeship (around 80% practical).

Centres of Expertise (19 in total) play a similar role to our Sector Skills Councils and advise on and agree the structure and content of vocational qualifications. There are currently more than 700 vocational qualifications which the Government aims to streamline to around 200.

Adult education runs independently alongside secondary vocational education. The Government does not fund leisure learning.

Strengths and Key Differences from the English System

Through the Centres of Expertise, there appears to be **more direct employer involvement** in determining the content and assessment of vocational qualifications.

Through the ROCs, there is **regional provision of backroom services**, including procurement, management information and planning. This provides considerable economies of scale and financial savings on administration. The ROC is block funded by the Ministry.

There is a very **flexible qualifications system** which focuses more specifically on skills and types of employment. Providers 'pick and mix' from the vocational qualification specification activities and processes which will provide young people with the appropriate knowledge and skills base. Each ROC and institution can deliver different sets of skills within the specification.

Although inspection is more frequent than in England (once every 3 years), the quality assurance system allows for **greater autonomy at institute level**.

Issues of Transferability for the FE College System

Employers are directly involved in determining the content and assessment of vocational courses. As a result, the Dutch curriculum has a strong vocational component. Employer contribution to curriculum design appears to raise the currency and status of vocational courses and qualifications.

Dutch teachers regularly update their industrial experience. This is seen as key to the success of learning delivery.

ONTARIO

Post secondary review: Ontario: A leader in learning

The honourable Bob Rae was appointed last year to advise on strategies to improve higher education in Ontario, Canada. He looked at the design and funding of the post compulsory sector, and reported in February 2005. His report states 'Ontario now has an opportunity to lead' and that this is a key mission. It states that the federal government must also become a reliable and steady partner in that mission. Leadership is needed to bring about change. His key recommendations are:

- Clarity in the mission of post compulsory institutions. The college mandate should be reaffirmed to focus on occupational education and labour market needs.

- Collaboration between universities and colleges. Opportunities for collaboration are being missed and there should be greater transparency and fairness in credit recognition between institutions.

- The pursuit of quality and innovation to make the student experience more rewarding.

- Opportunities for learning should be expanded to reach more people (including better information, participation targets and help for students with disabilities).

- Higher education should be more affordable.

- There should be capacity to meet growth priorities (including extra capital).

- There should be sustainable revenues for higher education including a new framework in which key partners – the government, institutions, students – each contribute in a responsible and predictable manner.

- Multi year plans setting out funding commitments to institutions.

- A council for higher education that would coordinate research, contribute to target setting and report on performance and outcomes. It would also advise on the evolution of the system.

- Better accountability for public funding. Self governance by institutions and institutional flexibility are important, but institutions should explain better what funding delivers. At the same time, government should not be too heavy handed or intrusive.

There are many similarities between the recommendations in the Ontario Review and the conclusions of this Review of the English FE college system.

APPENDIX 3: **OVERVIEW OF HOW WE WORKED**

Our aim has been to conduct this Review as openly as possible. We have consulted widely, meeting many people across the sector including learners and staff in colleges and inviting written evidence. We have also commissioned extensive new research that has yielded a rich bank of evidence from which to draw our analysis and recommendations. We give an overview here. Details of who we met, summaries of consultations and research and other evidence we gathered are available on the review website: www.dfes.gov.uk/ furthereducation/fereview.

The evidence and research we have collected is a valuable resource which is now available to policy and decision makers, those working in colleges and all other stakeholders. We hope people will use this resource to develop new ideas and ways of working and to inform future policy development.

CONSULTATION

At the beginning of the Review, we launched an **FE Review website** giving our terms of reference and outlining the processes we would be adopting.

In February 2005 we called for **written evidence** inviting views on the strengths, weaknesses and challenges facing the sector and asked about the key issues the Review should examine. We received over 270 responses in writing or through the website which

provided a huge amount of information and views that helped enormously in identifying the **10 key questions** we needed to address:

- What is the main purpose of further education colleges?

- How would you simplify and clarify the management and accountability system?

- How would you improve the learners' experience?

- How would you strengthen and improve the engagement with employers?

- How would you drive quality improvement for colleges?

- How would you develop corporate governance for colleges?

- How would you develop esteem in the sector and build its reputation?

- What are the most important aspects of the college workforce needs that must be attended to?

- What role should colleges play in developing the vocational pathways described in the 14-19 White Paper?

- How do we develop the leadership of the sector as well as leadership of colleges?

During June and July 2005 we asked for people's views on whether these were the right questions and, if so, what the answers should be. We received over 170 responses and the quality of thought and analysis in them was

impressive and added greatly to our analysis.

We held numerous **consultation meetings** with a whole range of stakeholders. We are grateful for the time people gave to us and for their frank and honest thoughts and views.

- **Over 100 individual meetings** with national and regional organisations including the DfES, LSC, AoC, Sixth Form College Forum, TUC, the main teaching unions, the inspectorates, QCA, HEFCE, Universities Vocational Council, Local Government Association, Secondary Heads Association, Sector Skills Councils, CBI and other employer organisations, ALP, RDAs, NIACE, and organisations representing particular interest groups (e.g. the Network of Black Managers and the Disability Rights Commission).

- **Meetings with groups of colleges** including representatives of sixth form colleges, specialist colleges, tertiary colleges, GFECs and various regional groupings.

- **Meetings with college staff and learners**: informal discussions on college visits (see below).

Around **20 consultation workshops** were held with different groups of stakeholders including learners, employers, college principals, governors, unions, independent providers, school leaders, the voluntary sector, LSC Chairs, higher education and the voluntary and community

FIGURE 9

Overview of consultation methods
We held numerous consultation meetings with a whole range of stakeholders.

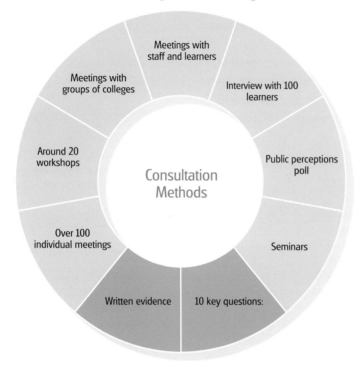

- Barton Peveril College, Hampshire
- Capel Manor College, Enfield
- Dearne Valley College, South Yorkshire
- Ealing, Hammersmith and West London College, London
- Hartpury College, Gloucestershire
- Newcastle College, Newcastle
- Plymouth College of Art and Design
- Telford College of Arts and Technology, Telford
- Stamford College, Stamford
- Waltham Forest College, London
- Warwickshire College, Leamington Spa
- The Working Men's College, London

We also visited some **independent providers** including Circa Ltd and Remploy.

RESEARCH

Throughout the Review we have gathered a huge amount of **new research**, including commissioning 15 short think pieces and some specific research. The think pieces covered:

- Structure and organisation of further education
- Mission purpose and specialisation
- The impact of incentives upon college behaviour
- Accountability, authority and leadership: a governance perspective
- Local management and leadership
- Authority and agency in general further education

sector. These enabled in depth and frank debate of the key issues affecting colleges and how to improve the learner experience. Around 160 people took part in these workshops.

Two formal discussion seminars hosted by external organisations were also held, one by the Institute of Public Policy Research and one by Open Agenda.

We **visited 12 colleges** across the country. We looked at the facilities and held discussions with the principal, senior management team, and met staff and learners. In some cases we looked at specific aspects of the college's work or facilities. We were very grateful for the time and effort colleges and their staff and learners gave to these visits. Colleges visited were:

- The role of further education in relation to equality, diversity and social inclusion

- The higher education role of further education colleges

- The untidy curriculum: adult learners in further education

- The curriculum for young people

- Staffing issues in FE

- The student experience of FE

- Culture and ethos

- Contestability in the learning and skills sector

- Exploring futures for FE to 2010

International comparisons were an important element of our work. We met with counterparts in Scotland (where we also visited a college) and Northern Ireland and visited 3 other countries, the United States, Denmark and the Netherlands to look at their systems, also visited a college in Gibralter. We also studied research and papers on a number of other countries' systems. Further information on the lessons learnt from international experience is given in appendix 2.

PUBLIC AND LEARNER PERCEPTIONS

In addition we were keen to find out more about how the wider population viewed FE colleges. We therefore commissioned MORI to conduct **a public perceptions** poll. They spoke to nearly 2,400 people, including learners, non-learners and parents during May and June 2005. The findings, outlined in section 3.5 of this report, gave us information on how people generally view FE colleges, how well they think

they fulfil their role and the barriers that stop them using college facilities.

And even more importantly we wanted to investigate **learners' perceptions** of colleges and their learning experience. In addition to the other consultations listed above we carried out a further piece of work involving **workshops and interviews with 100 learners**. We talked to young and adult learners and asked about the role FE colleges had played in their lives and what makes colleges successful in playing these roles. This provided a wealth of revealing and powerful information which is reflected in section 3.3 of this report. Many quotes from the learners involved are also spread throughout the report.

BRIEFINGS AND DATA

Briefing and data papers on specific issues and policies were requested from and prepared by DfES and LSC officials.

THE ADVISORY GROUP

The Review was supported by an Advisory Group. A list of members is in appendix 5.

THE REVIEW SECRETARIAT

A Secretariat drawn from the DfES and LSC has supported the Review, organising and coordinating consultations, meetings and other activity, commissioning research and undertaking many of the visits and meetings. They were:

DfES: Cynthia Hannah
       Andy Heath
       Victoria Nowell
       John Olivera
       Beth Simpson

LSC: Mary Heslop
       Ilona Murphy

APPENDIX 4: **FOSTER REVIEW: TERMS OF REFERENCE**

1. INTRODUCTION

The Government's Five Year Strategy sets out a vision which will have major implications for the future role and status of the Further Education sector.

In particular, the Government's reform plans for 14-19 and skills will require colleges in every community to examine their mission and relationship with other providers and learners / employers.

2. KEY REFORM AIMS

14-19

Through our 14-19 reforms we want colleges, working with other providers, to deliver to young people a much more personalised offer, including a wide choice of high quality vocational options.

Adult Skills

Through our Skills Strategy, we want colleges to be focused on and responsive to the skill needs of their local communities and of employers at local, regional and sectoral levels. The Strategy will involve individuals and employers making a greater investment in learning, particularly for higher level qualifications, with a particular focus for public investment on learners who need basic skills and their first level 2.

3. THE FOSTER REVIEW

Building on Success for All and the work of the LSC, Sir Andrew Foster will be asked to consider issues raised by the reform agenda for colleges of Further Education.

These will include:

a) Ethos, mission and structure;

b) Workforce, leadership and governance;

c) Relationships with other providers, schools and universities;

d) Employer engagement;

e) Business Planning and Income generation;

f) Systems to disseminate best practice and enhance the reputation of the sector.

It is envisaged the Review Group will publish its report in the Autumn of 2005.

APPENDIX 5: **ADVISORY GROUP**

We established an Advisory Group to advise on the key issues which the review should be addressing, and on the emerging themes and conclusions.

MEMBERSHIP:

George Bright,
Principal
Wiltshire College

Chris Clarke,
Headmaster
Queen Elizabeth School, Kirkby Lonsdale

Laurie Clarke/Dave Berger,
British Association for Counselling and Psychotherapy

Deborah Dale,
Voluntary & Community Sector Training Consortium (S. Yorkshire)

Martin Dunford,
TGB Learning & Training

Godfrey Glynn,
Principal
Barton Peveril Sixth Form College

Jill Hill,
Remploy UK Limited

Fran Hulbert,
North West Regional Development Agency

Chris Humphries CBE,
City and Guilds Awarding Body

Christine Lewis
Unison

Paul Mackney/Dan Taubman,
NATFHE

Professor David Melville CBE, Vice *Chancellor*
University of Kent

Bill Stokoe,
Former Chair of Corporation,
Ealing, Hammersmith & West London College

GLOSSARY AND QUALIFICATION LEVEL INDICATOR

GLOSSARY

Acronym	What does it stand for?
AACC	American Association of Community Colleges
ACM	Association for College Management
ALI	Adult Learning Inspectorate
ALP	Association of Learning Providers
AoC	Association of Colleges
BECTA	British Educational Communications and Technology Agency
CBI	Confederation of British Industry
CEL	Centre for Excellence in Leadership
CIF	Common Inspection Framework
CoVE	Centre of Vocational Excellence
CSR	Corporate Social Responsibility
DfES	Department for Education and Skills
E2E	Entry to Employment
EMS	Environmental Management Systems
ETP	Employer Training Pilot
FE	Further Education
FEFC	Further Education Funding Council
GCSE	General Certificate of Secondary Education
GFEC	General Further Education College
HE	Higher Education
HEFCE	Higher Education Funding Council for England
HESA	Higher Education Statistics Agency
LEA	Local Education Authority
LGA	Local Government Association
LLN	Lifelong Learning Network
LLSC	Local Learning and Skills Council
LLUK	Lifelong Learning UK
LSC	Learning and Skills Council
LSDA	Learning and Skills Development Agency
MIAP	Managing Information Across Partners
MSCHE	The Middle States Commission on Higher Education
NBM	Network for Black Managers
NDPB	Non Departmental Public Body
NETP	National Employer Training Programme
NHS	National Health Service
NIACE	National Institute for Adult Continuing Education
NQF	National Qualifications Framework
NSW	New South Wales
Ofsted	Office for Standards in Education
QAA	Quality Assurance Agency
QCA	Qualifications and Curriculum Authority
QIA	Quality Improvement Agency
RDA	Regional Development Agency
SFCF	Sixth Form College Forum
SHA	Secondary Heads Association
SSC	Sector Skills Council
TEC	Training and Enterprise Council
TUC	Trades Union Congress
ULR	Union Learning Representative
VET	Vocational Education and Training
WP	Widening Participation

QUALIFICATION LEVEL INDICATORS

Framework level	Level indicators	Examples of qualifications
Entry	Entry level qualifications recognise basic knowledge and skills and the ability to apply learning in everyday situations under direct guidance or supervision.	Qualifications are offered at entry 1, entry 2 and entry 3, in a range of subjects
Level 1	Level 1 qualifications recognise basic knowledge and skills and the ability to apply learning with guidance or supervision.	NVQ 1; Certificate in Plastering; GCSEs Grades D – G; Certificate in Motor Vehicle Studies
Level 2	Level 2 qualifications recognise the ability to gain a good knowledge and understanding of a subject area of work or study, and to perform varied tasks with some guidance or supervision.	NVQ 2; GCSEs Grades A* – C; Certificate in Coaching Football; Diploma for Beauty Specialists
Level 3	Level 3 qualifications recognise the ability to gain, and where relevant apply a range of knowledge, skills and understanding.	Certificate for Teaching Assistants; NVQ 3; A levels; Advanced Extension Awards; Certificate in Small Animal Care
Level 4	Level 4 qualifications recognise specialist learning and involve detailed analysis of a high level of information and knowledge in an area of work or study.	Diploma in Sport & Recreation; Certificate in Site Management; Certificate in Early Years Practice
Level 5	Level 5 qualifications recognise the ability to increase the depth of knowledge and understanding of an area of work or study to enable the formulation of solutions and responses to complex problems and situations.	Diploma in Construction; Certificate in Performing Arts
Level 6	Level 6 qualifications recognise a specialist high level knowledge of an area of work or study to enable the use of an individual's own ideas and research in response to complex problems and situations.	Certificate or Diploma in Management
Level 7	Level 7 qualifications recognise highly developed and complex levels of knowledge which enable the development of in-depth and original responses to complicated and unpredictable problems and situations.	Diploma in Translation; Fellowship in Music Literacy
Level 8	Level 8 qualifications recognise leading experts or practitioners in a particular field.	Specialist awards

Source: http://www.qca.org.uk/493.html